WHAT TO EXPECT FROM FLIGHT TRAINING! WHEN YOU WANT TO BECOME A COMMERCIAL PILOT

THE OVERALL PROCESS OF FLIGHT TRAINING AND OBTAINING PILOT CERTIFICATES EXPLAINED

VESA TURPEINEN

CONTENTS

A SPECIAL FREE GIFT FOR YOU!

As a THANK YOU for purchasing my book, I would like to give you FREE instant access to some bonus materials. The bonus materials include the following:

- Phonetic Alphabet for Pilots — Cheatsheet.
- Decoding Guide for METAR and TAF Weather Reports

Details at the end of the book. Enjoy the flight!

Copyright & Disclaimer

INTRODUCTION

"It is possible to fly without motors, but not without knowledge and skill."
— *Wilbur Wright*

This quote, from one of the fathers of modern aviation, still holds true today. You don't necessarily need motors to fly — think of gliders, for example. But you can't fly safely without knowledge and skills. Each pilot knows it takes a lot of study and practice to become a professional aviator. Training provides you the necessary skills to fly safely. Nobody is born a pilot, and you can't fly an airplane with instincts only.

All professional pilots start as student pilots working

towards a private pilot license. Next, you would need to add an instrument rating to the license, while then moving onto commercial pilot training.

In commercial pilot training, you would usually get a single-engine commercial pilot license first and add a multi-engine rating to the permit later. The process varies between training schools, though; in some cases, you might not even get a single-engine commercial license at all. Instead, you might only get the multi-engine license.

Some training programs additionally include flight instructor training after the commercial pilot training, so that you can graduate as a flight instructor at the end of the course.

Getting all these certificates and ratings involves rigorous training in the air and the classroom. It also includes taking many written and practical examinations before you can move onto the next phase of training.

If you read the first book of these series – *"Learn to Fly and Become a Pilot!"* – then you already know my story. I won't repeat it here. Although, I will mention that I worked as a flight instructor, while later working as a chief flight instructor of a major flight academy for many years. I trained hundreds of students, who all progressed through a similar process described in this book. Since my flight instructor days, I have been working as a corporate pilot flying private business jets. My career has been very rewarding. In my books, I'm excited to share with you all the knowledge I have gained from working in aviation.

My first book explained; what it takes to become a pilot, available career options for pilots, how to choose a flight school, how to finance the training, etc. Presuming you followed the steps provided at the end of the book, you have probably: chosen your flight training school, applied for a student pilot license, and completed your pilot medical examination. Now you should be looking forward to starting your flight training in the following weeks or months.

Even after all that preparation, you might still only have a vague idea about what the training process entails. Technically, there is nothing wrong with that. You are not required to have any previous aviation knowledge when you join a pilot training program. But the more you know in advance, the easier your time at the flight school will be. This, too, can translate into savings. This is because your examinations will be easier to pass. And, it's unlikely you'll need any extra training if you are well-prepared for each lesson.

This book is here to help you understand what flight training is all about. Keep on reading.

ABOUT THIS BOOK

This is the second book of the *Pilot Career Series*. If you have not yet committed to flight training, I recommend you first read book one.[1] Then come back to this book. Unless you know a career as a pilot is a good fit for you, there is no point to learn about the training process itself.

When I started my flight training, I had no clue about what to expect from my time at the flight school regarding the studies. It was quite nerve-racking to travel across the Atlantic Ocean (from Finland to the United States) for flight training when I wasn't sure what exactly was it all about. At the time, I didn't really care. I knew that I would become a commercial pilot by the end of the course.

Thinking back, I wish I had studied a bit in advance. That would have made my life a lot easier during those first few months at the school. Also, if I had known what I know today, I could have finished my training faster and saved some money on instructor fees and aircraft rental fees.

This is the book I wish I had read before my first day of flight training. In this book, I will give you a better idea of what to expect from each stage of your training. When you know what is expected from you in advance, you can better prepare for your training. Moreover, you can be confident that you will smoothly progress through the course.

This book will explain the aeronautical topics, maneuvers, and other training requirements that you will learn during each phase of training. The topics are not covered in detail, but links to free Federal Aviation Administration (FAA) manuals will be provided. Therefore, you can get detailed information on each subject if desired.

The FAA publications cover each aeronautical knowledge area and maneuver in detail, which is why it would make no sense for me to cover the same information here. The amount of the free publications can be overwhelming, so I will point you to specific publications and chapters when needed.

Instead of focusing on the details of each individual topic, the purpose of this book is to give you a quick overview of what you can expect from your flight training.

You are in the right place no matter what aviation career path you are interested in. Different career paths were described in book one of these series. These include corporate pilots, airline pilots, flight instructors, etc. Every pilot goes through the same or similar process that's described in this book.

Although, I will only cover the training in-depth up to a commercial pilot license. It's all essential information in your journey towards an airline pilot license, which is briefly covered at the end of the book.

Throughout the book there are little endnote marks such as this: [2]. The endnotes indicate links to different resources. You can find all the links at the end of the book from the "notes". For your convenience, I have also compiled all the links in one location on my resources page at https://www.funkypilot.com/resources[3], so you can easily visit them after you have finished the book.

All the links have been checked during the time of this writing, and will be re-checked occasionally. However, if you find a link that's not working, please let me know by e-mail: vesa.turpeinen@funkypilot.com.

Another resource that is located at the end of the book is a glossary. Aviation is full of abbreviations and acronyms that are commonly used among pilots, air traffic controllers (ATC), and other aviation personnel. In this book alone, I use over 50 aviation abbreviations or acronyms. All of them are spelled out initially, but for subsequent usage, you can quickly refresh you memory by looking at the glossary.

Please, send me an email if you have any questions once you have read the book. I'll answer whenever I'm not flying.

Good luck with your training!

NOTE TO MY INTERNATIONAL READERS:

The information in this book mostly applies to flight training in the United States, following regulations set by the FAA. However, you can still benefit from reading this book even if you're planning to do your training in another country.

Flight training in most countries follow a similar pattern; you get the exact same licenses in the same order. Most of the aeronautical knowledge areas and flight maneuvers will be the same as well. And there will be practical examinations at the end of each training course, regardless of your aviation authority.

There are some differences, though:

For example, the FAA requires only one knowledge

exam for each pilot certification or rating, while EASA (European Aviation Safety Agency) requires several exams for each license. I am currently in the process of getting my EASA ATPL (Airline Transport Pilot License), which requires me to take fourteen knowledge exams in different subjects. My FAA and CAAC (Civil Aviation Administration of China) ATP licenses only required me to take one exam each, a big difference. If you learn to fly in Europe, you are likely to spend a lot more time studying for knowledge exams than in the United States.

However, in the United States, you will still spend time to study the theory. Your knowledge will be tested in a different way. The FAA requires an oral exam as part of each practical examination. In an oral exam, a designated FAA examiner will ask you questions about each aeronautical topic necessary for your license. Oral exams can be very stressful and can take anything from less than an hour to several hours, depending on the examiner.

Despite the differences, the overall process of flight training, ground school studies, taking written exams, and taking practical examinations will be the same. This book will help you get the overall picture of what to expect from flight training, regardless of your location.

OVERVIEW OF PILOT CERTIFICATES AND RATINGS

To become a professional pilot, you need to obtain several different pilot certificates and ratings. There is usually a separate training course required for each certificate or rating. You will also have to take separate knowledge and practical exams at the end of each course.

In this Chapter, I will give you a brief overview of the certificates and ratings that are available for airplane pilots. Much of this chapter is a review from the first book of these series, but I believe it's good to take a quick look at each certificate before we dig into the details.

Pilot certificates and ratings required from a professional pilot are the following:

PILOT CERTIFICATES

- **Student pilot certificate**: Required for solo flight training, and used to keep track of people receiving flight training. It has no expiration date, and you can get it for free before you even start your training.

- **Private pilot certificate (PPL)**: Allows you to fly a rental or privately-owned airplane with passengers. However, you are not allowed to earn money for the flights. Private pilot certificates are primarily meant for recreational flying or personal transportation.

- **Commercial pilot certificate (CPL)**: Required for you to fly for compensation or hire. This is it! Once you get your commercial pilot certificate, you can call yourself a professional pilot! And, of course, this is when you can start applying for pilot jobs that pay you cold hard cash!

- **Airline transport pilot certificate (ATPL)**: The commercial pilot certificate can help you go far in your career, but at some point you will need to get your ATPL if you want to work in certain airline and passenger carrying operations.

Are they Certificates or a Licenses?

Notice that I use the term 'certificate' instead of a 'license.' That's because the FAA calls them pilot certificates. In other countries, they are usually called pilot licenses. Also, you will hear people talking about PPL training or CPL training. Here they are referring to a private pilot license or a commercial pilot license. It's the authorizing document you need to operate an aircraft with certain privileges and limitations. In this book, I use the terms license and certificate interchangeably.

PILOT RATINGS

Ratings are additional authorizations that set forth special conditions, privileges, or limitations for your pilot certificate or license. There are basically three ratings you can have added to your pilot certificate. If you want to make flying your career, you should strive for at least two of them.

- **Instrument Rating (IR)**: This is a **must-get** rating. Every professional pilot needs to have an instrument rating. Normally, this is acquired after you earn your private pilot certificate, and will be automatically transferred to your commercial pilot certificate once you get it. Instrument rating allows you to fly in low visibilities and through clouds. Even private pilots should get this rating, as the training alone will make you a safer and more skilled pilot.

- **Multi-Engine Rating:** This is the second rating you should get added to your pilot certificate if you want to fly for a living. Without a multi-engine rating, you are limited to flying only single-engine airplanes. You can get by with single-engine planes for a while if you work as a flight instructor or take passengers up on sightseeing flights. You could even fly those single-engine Cessna Caravans, taking passengers from island-to-island in Hawaii. But overall, you will be very limited in terms of your job opportunities. Most airlines operate multi-engine airplanes, so just get the multi-engine rating!

- **Seaplane Rating (Single-Engine and/or Multi-Engine; Optional):** Seaplane ratings are optional ratings for most pilots. There are relatively few commercial operators that use seaplanes for transportation (or any other operations). You won't be doing any long-distance piloting with seaplanes, but they are a lot of fun to fly. I only have a few hours in seaplanes, and I only have the single-engine seaplane rating. But it was still some of the most fun flying I have ever done.

INSTRUCTOR CERTIFICATES AND RATINGS (Optional)

Although all flight instructors are pilots, the authorizing certificate for a flight instructor is not a pilot certificate; there is a separate instructor certificate. The prerequisite for getting an instructor certificate is having a commercial pilot or airline transport pilot certificate.

You don't need to become a flight instructor if you think you can find another type of commercial pilot job after you finish your flight training.

However, I would recommend you consider working as a flight instructor before you start your passenger transportation career. You will be surprised how much you will learn from teaching students. Working as a flight instructor for a year or two will give you a good base of knowledge before you move on to better-paying pilot jobs.

The instructor certificates and ratings are:

- **Certified Flight Instructor (CFI) Certificate**: Required to teach students at the private and commercial pilot level. This also allows you to train other flight instructors for their initial flight instructor certification. The initial instructor certification is normally completed in a single-engine aircraft, so you will be limited to teaching only single-engine students— even if you have a multi-engine rating on your commercial pilot certificate.

- **Certified Flight Instructor Instrument (CFII) Rating**: Required to teach instrument rating students or instrument instructors. Instrument flying is such an important skill that you will need a separate instrument rating on your instructor certificate, even if you already have an instrument rating on your commercial pilot certificate.

- **Certified Flight Instructor Multi-Engine (MEI) Rating**: Required to teach students in an aircraft that has more than one engine. With this rating you can instruct students for the initial multi-engine rating or multi-engine instructor rating.

GROUND INSTRUCTOR CERTIFICATES (Optional)

Ground instructors are basically teachers who are allowed to teach aviation knowledge to students. They are also allowed to endorse students to take their FAA knowledge exams.

You don't need to be a pilot to become a ground instructor. And working as a ground instructor doesn't involve flying, instead you would be teaching aviation knowledge to pilot students.

The reason I mention these certificates is that they are very easy to obtain while you are studying for the other certificates, and they can be useful to you later in life (especially if you decide to work at a flight school someday).

There will be some ground training and written knowledge exams involved in getting these certificates, but no practical exams will be required.

Ground instructor certificates are issued without an expiration date, so they can be a good insurance policy in case you lose your pilot medical certificate for some reason.

There is always a need for educators, so it shouldn't be too difficult for you to find a job as a ground instructor if necessary. Ground instructor certificates will help you share your aviation knowledge if you have to stop flying someday.

There are three different levels of ground instructor certificates:

- **Basic Ground Instructor (BGI)**:
  Required to provide ground instruction for sport, recreational, and private pilot students.

- **Advanced Ground Instructor (AGI)**:
  Required to provide ground training for all other pilot certificates, except the instrument rating.

- **Instrument Ground Instructor (IGI)**: Required to provide ground training for the instrument rating.

Wasn't that some list? The good news: you don't need them all to have a rewarding career as a professional pilot. You also don't need to worry about them all at once.

Instead, you will focus on one pilot certificate and maybe one pilot rating at a time. You will be following a step-by-step training program that's designed to teach you new things in a logical order. The new things that you learn are based on previously learned material, which is why it's crucial you thoroughly understand what you are being taught at all stages of training.

If you don't understand something, ask your instructor or other students. You can even send me an e-mail regarding any flight training questions.

While there are many optional certificates and ratings, you need at least a commercial pilot license with an instrument rating if you want to make flying your career. Next, I will describe the process of obtaining eacd certificate and rating – one at the time.

STUDENT PILOT CERTIFICATE - FAR 61 SUBPART C

The first pilot certificate you need to obtain is called a student pilot certificate.[1] You don't need it to take flight or ground lessons, but you will need it before your first solo flight. The process of obtaining it was explained in *"Pilot Career Book One."* So, I'll make it brief here.

This Chapter is the shortest chapter in the book, because there is no training involved in getting a student pilot certificate.

To be eligible for a student pilot certificate, you need to be sixteen years old. You must be able to read, write, and understand the English language. There are no other requirements set forth by the FAA.

How to apply for it?

You can apply for the student pilot certificate through the Integrated Airman Certification and Rating Application (IACRA).[2] Simply fill all the required information on the online application; although, you need someone to verify your identity before submitting the application. That someone needs to be an FAA-certified flight instructor, a designated pilot examiner, or an employee at a Flight Standards District Office (FSDO). Once this person has verified your identity, you can submit the electronic form.

Your certificate will be mailed to you within about three weeks. There is no fee or expiration date for a student pilot certificate. Therefore, there is no reason not to get it early. Don't wait until you actually start training. Get it as soon as possible since you need it before your first solo flight. If you do accelerated flight training, you might be ready for your first solo within a week of your first flight lesson.

The first actual pilot certificate for which you need to train is the private pilot certificate. Next I will discuss the process of obtaining that.

PRIVATE PILOT CERTIFICATE - FAR 61 SUBPART E AND FAR 141 APPENDIX B

Once you have your student pilot certificate, medical certificate, and a government-issued ID, you possess all the required documents for obtaining a private pilot license.

All pilots start their careers by becoming private pilots first. This is when you learn basic stick and rudder skills. You learn how to operate an aircraft manually without an autopilot, and there is no way around it.

A private pilot certificate is the first actual pilot certificate you need to obtain. The student pilot certificate doesn't count because there are no skills involved in getting it.

Getting the private pilot certificate is perhaps the most important part of your flight training, because it validates your capabilities of becoming a pilot.

This Chapter is the longest chapter of the book, and will cover everything you can expect from private pilot training.

Private Pilot Training Requirements

All private pilot training requirements can be found within the Federal Aviation Regulations (FAR) Part 61, Subpart E and Part 141, Appendix B. (That's why it's in the Chapter title). In general, the training consists of ground training and flight training.

The requirements that apply to you are based on whether you train at an FAR Part 61 or Part 141 school. I explained what the federal aviation regulations are and the differences between those two pilot schools in my previous book, but since I will be comparing the requirements of the two different school types a lot in this book, a brief explanation as a reminder is in order.

The 'parts' that I'm talking about refer to the different parts of the Code of Federal Regulations (CFR), which is the codification of the general and permanent rules published by different government agencies.

The CFR itself is a huge document, consisting of 50 broad category sections that are called 'titles'. Title 14 of the

CFR is called "Aeronautics and Space," and is also known as the Federal Aviation Regulations (or FARs), which are published by the Federal Aviation Administration (FAA).

Learning about the different FARs is an essential part of your flight training. Everything we do in the air is structured to follow certain rules that are designed to keep us (and everyone below us) safe. Title 14 of the CFR includes those rules, and is further divided into several parts that describe the regulations for particular aspects of aviation.

You can access all the regulations from www. ecfr.gov for free. Simply choose Title 14 from the main menu, and then navigate to any of the parts you want to study.

Parts 61 and 141 refer to sections of the Federal Aviation Regulations in the Title 14 of the CFR.

Flight schools in the United States either operate under FAR Part 61 or Part 141 rules.

In general, Part 141 schools provide training that is structured according to FAA guidelines, while Part 61 training is more relaxed. Because of the relaxed rules that apply to Part 61 schools, their students are required to log more total flight training hours than students at Part 141 schools.

The opposite is true about ground training, however; as you keep reading, you will see that Part 141 schools require a lot of ground training from their students, while in Part 61 schools there are no specific ground training requirements.

Although the rules between the schools differ, you will need to demonstrate identical knowledge and skills, whether you train at a Part 61 or Part 141 school.

Private Pilot Ground Training

There are several different aeronautical knowledge areas on which you will be tested on at the end of the private pilot training course.

The knowledge areas are the same for both schools; the difference being 141 schools require a minimum of thirty-five hours for ground training, which covers these areas.

There are no specific time requirements if you train in a 61 school. You just need to receive training in the required knowledge areas. Alternatively, in 61 schools, you could skip the ground school altogether, completing a home-study course instead.

There are online-based home-study courses available that can prepare you for the required knowledge exam. Completing the course before you start flight training could potentially save a lot of time and money with your training because you could focus on flying full-time. More about the home-study courses later.

Part 141 Ground School

The thirty-five-hour requirement by 141 schools is not really that much when you think about it. You could complete it all within a week or in five days; that is if you study seven hours a day for five days straight.

In spite of this, most schools will break it down a bit. It may be too much information to digest in such a short period of time. And, you will need study time so that you can complete some homework on your own.

It's important for you to have some aviation knowledge before you start your flight lessons, but it's not necessary to complete the whole ground course before you start to fly.

In 141 schools you might be taking ground school classes and flight lessons at the same time. Normally you will learn the necessary aviation knowledge to pass the

FAA knowledge exam from ground school, while your personal flight instructor will prepare you for each flight lesson.

Overall, everything should be well organized in 141 schools. You will appropriately be guided through all your training. As long as you go with the flow and follow the FAA-approved training program, you should meet all the training requirements by the end of each course.

Then, you will get your private pilot certificate within a specific time frame. Mistakes, of course, can happen. So, make sure you and your instructor will carefully complete all required training records after each flight and ground lesson. It's also good if you keep track of your training progress yourself, thereby making sure you don't miss any requirements.

Part 61 Ground School

While in a Part 61 school, you will have more responsibility to take care of your training records and make sure you cover each required subject. Since there is no hourly requirement for ground school training, the school may not provide you with a training syllabus to follow.

Instead, you and your flight instructor may have to keep track of each subject without any standardized guidance from the school. Most schools, however, follow some sort of syllabus even though it's not a requirement.

Therefore, while training at a 61 Part school, it would be a good idea to study as much as possible before you start flying. Even better, complete the PPL knowledge exam before you start flying, so your focus is on flight training. More about the knowledge exam in the next section.

Regardless of the school you attend, you should have some basic aviation knowledge before you start your flight lessons. The more you know before actually beginning to fly, the easier it is to learn and grasp the required skills while you are flying.

For example, knowing about the functions of basic aircraft instruments or basic aerodynamical principles before your first flight lesson will make the flight more enjoyable. You can then focus on controlling the aircraft instead of trying to figure out what all the dials and gauges are supposed to mean.

Ground School Topics

Although, the hour requirements differ in 61 and 141 schools, they both require you to receive and log ground training on certain aeronautical knowledge areas.

Alternatively, you could complete an authorized home study course on the same knowledge areas:

1. Applicable Federal Aviation Regulations (FAR) that relate to private pilot privileges, limitations, and flight operations.
2. Accident reporting requirements of the National Transportation Safety Board (NTSB).
3. Use of applicable portions of the Aeronautical Information Manual (AIM) and FAA advisory circulars.
4. Use of aeronautical charts for VFR navigation using pilotage, dead reckoning, and navigation systems.
5. Radio communication procedures.
6. Recognition of critical weather situations from the ground and in flight. Additionally, this includes wind-shear avoidance, and the procurement and use of aeronautical weather reports and forecasts.
7. Safe and efficient operation of an aircraft, including collision avoidance, and recognition and avoidance of wake turbulence.

8. Effects of density altitude on takeoff and climb performance.

9. Weight and balance computations.

10. Principles of aerodynamics, power plants, and aircraft systems.

11. Stall awareness, spin entry, spins, and recovery techniques.

12. Aeronautical decision-making and judgment.

13. Pre-flight action that includes:

14. How to obtain information on runway lengths at airports of intended use; data on takeoff and landing distances; weather reports and forecasts; and fuel requirements.

15. How to plan for alternatives if the planned flight cannot be completed or delays are encountered.

Wow! That's an intimidating list of stuff! They are all very broad areas of knowledge. But don't worry. I will break it down for you in a bit. And, they'll break it down further in ground school. If you study on your own, you can simply study one section at the time.

Let's look at each subject in more detail:

1. Applicable FARs that relate to private pilot privileges, limitations, and flight operations.

If you read the first book of these series, you already know a bit about the FARs. You can read them for free from the Electronic Code of Federal Regulations (eCFR).[1]

The regulations you need to know as a private pilot can be found from 14 CFR Part 61, Subpart C and E.[2] If you train in a 141 school, you will further need to know regulations from FAR 141, Appendix B.[3]

In general, part 61 and 141 regulations describe the training requirements, privileges, limitations, etc. for each pilot certificate and rating.

Knowing the applicable regulations is very important for pilots. Violating any rules or regulations, whether intentionally or unintentionally, may in some cases mean the end of your career. Reading the regulations can be very daunting. It may feel pointless at times, which is why you need to put some conscious effort into studying them.

During your private pilot training, you will learn about the privileges and limitations applicable to student and private pilots. Your basic privileges as a private pilot are to act as the pilot in command of a private aircraft.

You are not allowed to fly for compensation or hire; although, there are a few exceptions.

You will also learn about the experience and training requirements for obtaining a private pilot certificate. This is important knowledge to learn at this stage, but it's not something you will need to remember later on during your career.

I mean, why would an airline captain care about the flight hour requirements for obtaining a private pilot certificate? That's right; they don't.

The same thing concerns student pilot limitations. You won't need to remember them once you have your private pilot license. Many of the regulations only apply to your current stage of training. But you may have to remember other rules, such as instrument currency requirements or commercial pilot privileges, for the rest of your career.

While you won't go into the instrument or commercial regulations during your private pilot training, you will learn some essential rules that you will always have to remember.

What is FAR Part 91?

Some of the most important regulations can be found from FAR Part 91 - General Operating and Flight

Rules.[4] They are the operating rules which all pilots have to follow.

It doesn't matter whether you are a private pilot, commercial pilot, or an airline transport pilot. You will need to know these rules. Still, some of the rules that you need to follow will depend on the type of flight operations you conduct.

If you take a look at the FAR Part 91, you will notice there are a lot of rules. It starts at 91.1 and ends at 91.1721! Don't worry, though; you won't have to study them all, at least for now! And there are actually not that many regulations; there is a lot of reserved space for future additions.

For example, in the Subpart A, regulations 91.27 - 91.99 are all blank. All the regulations before 91.27 are odd-numbered, meaning there are only thirteen numbered regulations in Part 91, Subpart A. And, there are fourteen subparts in Part 91.

Still seems like a lot?

For now, you will only need to study the "applicable" regulations – meaning the rules that apply to your stage of pilot training. During private pilot training, you will roughly need to study the Part 91 rules from Subpart A to E. You can skip most of the instrument and special flight operations that don't apply to you at this stage.

In ground school you will learn what you should be focusing on. But for now, I can mention that the important stuff is in Subpart B – Flight Rules. Those are the rules you need to follow when you are flying. You need to know by heart all the rules of the air, because you won't have time to browse through the regulations while you are flying.

2. Accident reporting requirements of the NTSB

Normally, you won't spend too much time in this subject area. While it's important to know about accident reporting requirements, it's something most pilots will never actually have to do. I remember reviewing the accident reporting requirements many, many times during my career. Nonetheless, I have never actually had any practical need for the knowledge. Thank goodness!

If you have an accident or an incident, you can always go online and find out the details on how, where, and when to report the event.

However, you need to be aware of the accident and incident reporting requirements set forth by the

National Transportation Safety Board (NTSB). You will have to read through and study the section from the Code of Federal Regulations (CFR) Title 49: Transportation. The part you need to study is 49 CFR Part 830,[5] which talks about the notification and reporting of aircraft incidents and accidents.

More regulations. Having fun with flight training yet?? Oh, don't worry. Part 830 is only a few pages long, and you'll breeze through it quickly. Just make sure you understand the regulations. Then, focus on studying more important things that will keep you away from accidents!

3. Use of applicable portions of the AIM and FAA advisory circulars

The Aeronautical Information Manual (AIM) is an official guide manual published by the FAA. It's designed to provide the aviation community with basic flight information and air traffic control procedures for use in the National Airspace System (NAS) of the United States.

If you fly in the United States, you need to know and understand the information contained in this manual. Just like all FAA publications, you can download AIM for free. You can find a download link to it and over thirty other FAA manuals at my resources page: funkyp-ilot.com/resources.[6]

The PDF version of the book is a fairly massive 780-page opus. But again, you just need to know the applicable portions of the manual. You need to learn airport and airspace operations for sure; however, you don't need to worry about things such as instrument navigation at this stage.

So what are advisory circulars?

Advisory Circulars (or ACs) are informational documents issued by the FAA. They are meant to give guidance and clarify different issues within the aviation industry. They are often used to explain regulations that may otherwise be difficult to interpret. There are tons of them out there, and during your training, your ground instructor will point out the ones applicable to you.

Advisory circulars are intended to be informative in nature and not regulatory. However, after studying them, it's good to follow the advice. They often describe actions or advice that the FAA expects to be implemented or followed. And since they are often used to explain regulations, a lot of the information is, in fact, regulatory.

As an example of an advisory circular, you should

take a look at AC 61.65H Certification: Pilots and Flight and Ground Instructors.[7] It provides guidance for pilot and instructor applicants. You will quickly notice that it's fifty-eight pages of really dry reading, but there is a table of contents so you can quickly jump to a part that applies to you. In any case, it's a good AC to keep for reference as you progress through your training.

FAA maintains a massive database of advisory circulars that you can browse at the FAA website.[8] They are categorized by topic, which allows you to find the ones that apply to you or interest you easily.

4. Use of aeronautical charts for VFR navigation using pilotage, dead reckoning, and navigation systems

Navigation is a very important topic for obvious reasons. You wouldn't want to get lost while flying a plane and running low on fuel! The reason for most flying is to travel from point A to point B; and, there are many ways you can navigate between the points.

During your private pilot training, you are not allowed to fly through clouds or in low visibility. Instead, you will learn to fly in a Visual Meteorological Conditions (VMC). It has different definitions based on the airspace in which you operate, but in general, you will need at least five nautical miles of visibility and stay clear of clouds when you fly in VMC.

VFR navigation means navigation using visual flight rules. You will hear many people using VMC and VFR interchangeably. People will say it's VFR outside, although the correct term would be VMC. It's no big deal because the ultimate meaning is the same. In VMC, you could still fly by following the Instrument Flight Rules (IFR), but it doesn't work the other way around. You can't fly using visual flight rules in instrument meteorological conditions (IMC).

When you study VFR navigation, you will learn how to read and use VFR charts. Basically, they are colorful maps used for visual navigation. Before each flight, you study those maps to find easily recognizable ground reference points along your planned route. During a flight, you find those reference points by looking out the window and compare your aircraft position to your planned route on the map.

You will also learn how to navigate by pilotage and dead reckoning. These terms are probably new to you, so I'll explain. Pilotage is a navigation method in which you fly from checkpoint to checkpoint by visual reference to objects on the ground. You may, for example, follow a highway from one small town to the next. Or you can use large intersections, towers, lakes, or anything else easily recognizable as your checkpoints.

Dead reckoning is a navigation method in which you will calculate your headings and speeds based on expected wind conditions before the flight.

Then, during the flight, you follow your calculated headings. These should make you fly a certain ground track. You won't be blindly trusting your calculations, for pilotage and dead reckoning are normally used together for cross-country navigation.

Therefore, you would also calculate your estimated times over each check point and your expected fuel burn as part of your dead reckoning calculations. Then, you will keep a record of your heading, time, fuel burn, etc. over each checkpoint. And you make adjustments when necessary.

Within this topic, you will further learn about electronic instrument navigation systems such as the Global Positioning System (GPS), Very-High Frequency Omni-Directional Range (VOR), and Non-Directional Radio Beacon (NDB).

You won't spend much time studying instrument navigation at this stage though. But you will learn the basics of how to use the the navigational instruments installed in your training aircraft.

You will cover all these aspects of navigation in the

classroom before you start your actual cross-country flight training.

5. Radio communication procedures

Radio communication is another extremely important subject. You need to be able to communicate with the air traffic controllers (ATC) as well as other pilots in the air. During your private pilot training, you will learn all the basic radio calls and communication procedures for VFR flying. For example, you will learn the phonetic alphabet and other radio phraseology that you will be using in the air. This is something you can easily study before you even start your training. The phonetic alphabet is included in the bonus materials that come with this book.

It takes time and practice to get proficient with radio talk. If you are like me, and English is your second language, talking on the radio can feel very intimidating at first. It can be hard finding the words you want to say. But don't worry, for it will get easier over time. To make it easier for yourself, you can have the correct radio phrases written down on your notepad when you first start flying. That can be a good reminder of what to say. That's what I did when I was doing my private pilot training.

AOPA has published a very useful cheatsheet with sample radio calls for airplanes departing and arriving different classes of airspaces. You can download it from their website (see the endnote)[9], and use it as a reference during your training. Simply replace the callsigns, airport names, and other essential information with information that apply to your training.

6. Recognition of critical weather situations from the ground and in flight, wind-shear avoidance, and the procurement and use of aeronautical weather reports and forecasts

Knowledge of weather theory and aviation weather services is a big part of your ground school training. Every flight starts by checking the local weather, en-route weather, and forecasted weather at your arrival airport. A good place to start studying weather is the Pilot's Handbook of Aeronautical Knowledge (PHAK). You can download it for free from my resources page.[10] It's an FAA handbook that contains a massive amount of information. Instead of reading it from cover to cover, you can pick the chapters relevant to you at the time. PHAK chapter twelve[11] talks about weather theory, and chapter thirteen[12] talks about aviation weather services.

One thing I want to mention about the weather

reports – specifically aviation weather reports provided to pilots – is that these are not written in plain language. They're not like when you listen to a weather report in the news. Instead, they are provided using certain codes that make the reports much shorter than they would be if written in plain language. Learning the weather codes is very important for pilots because you need to check the weather before every flight.

For example, the following is a standard meteorological weather report or a METAR for JFK airport in New York:

METAR: KJFK 050251Z 35009KT 10SM FEW050 BKN250 25/21 A2995

Below is a terminal area forecast for Daytona Beach airport in Florida:

TAF: KDAB 042331Z 0500/0524 26018G25KT P6SM FEW045 FM051400 27017G25KT

· · ·

These are examples of very basic weather reports you will learn to decode. You need to be able to read the weather before each flight. It will make your life easier in the classroom if you learn how to read them in advance.

The reports essentially tell you the wind speed and direction at the airport, outside visibility, cloud coverage, temperature and dew point, altimeter setting, etc. I made a cheat-sheet that you can use to decode METAR and TAF reports. You can download it using the link at the end of the book.

7. Safe and efficient operation of aircraft, including collision avoidance, and recognition and avoidance of wake turbulence

"Safety First." Everyone has heard that saying regarding just about anything you do. When you do flight training, safety is emphasized in every stage of training. It's good to pay attention to safety practices starting from the beginning of your training. Carry them throughout your career so that you can have a long accident and incident-free career.

Collision avoidance procedures in private pilot flying are important. You need to be constantly scanning outside visually for other aircraft. You will learn to clear the area before each turn you make by looking at all directions before turning. This is especially important in the United States, where there is lots of VFR traffic who might not be talking to any air traffic controllers.

Regarding collision avoidance, you will also learn the right of way rules in the air and the ground, and how to keep safe distances to other aircraft in the air, etc.

When you fly small planes, you need to be extra careful about wake turbulence created by bigger airplanes. There are many records of accidents caused by wake turbulence from other aircraft. You will learn all about the recommended distances and times before taking off or landing after heavy jets. You will also learn about the movements of wake turbulence based on wind speed and direction. Wake turbulence may affect you even if you are taking off from a different runway than the previous aircraft.

8. Effects of density altitude on takeoff and climb performance

There are thousands of airports around the world. Most of them are located near the sea level where the air is denser, which provides better performance for aircraft engines. Although, many airports are located in higher elevations.

The airport in Lhasa, Tibet, for example, is located at an altitude of 11,710 feet. Air at that altitude is less dense than at sea-level. With less dense air, the aircraft performance decreases. Therefore, the aircraft operating in and out of high altitude airports have to consider the performance effects of the altitude very carefully.

The outside-air temperature has a similar effect on aircraft performance. Higher temperature reduces the performance of airplanes, meaning you would need more runway taking off. Also, the aircraft, as a result, would climb at a slower rate after takeoff.

Performance can be a complex subject for many. You will have to use some math here, but no worries. You don't need to be a math expert. You will learn all the required calculations in your ground school. To do these calculations, you will learn to use either a digital or mechanical flight computer that is specially made for aviation calculations.

Although they are called computers, they are more like calculator-sized devices. Nowadays, you could do all the calculations with smart-phone apps, but unfortunately, you are not allowed to bring a smart-phone or tablet when you take any FAA exam. So, you better get one of the approved flight computers. You can check out my resources page[13] for different models of flight computers.

To calculate your performance for any given airport, you will learn to read aircraft performance charts and airport charts to find important information such as the airport elevation, runway lengths, runway slopes, etc. By now, you should be familiar with weather concepts such as pressure altitude and density altitude. When you study performance, you will see how weather can affect your takeoff and climb performance.

9. Weight and Balance computations

In addition to checking the weather and making performance calculations, weight and balance computations are also done before each flight. Normally you will cover the weight and balance calculations in ground school first, and review them with your personal flight instructor later.

It's essential to learn the calculations for the type of aircraft which you will use during your training. You will have to calculate weight and balance for each flight, either doing it with your instructor or alone. Normally your flight instructor will review how to do it before your first flight lesson.

By weight and balance calculations, I mean calculating your takeoff and landing weights, as well as the aircraft center of gravity. The weights are different because of the fuel burn. Knowing the weights are important for calculating your takeoff and landing distances as well as climb performance after takeoff. You must make sure your aircraft will be at or below the maximum takeoff weight.

You need to calculate the center of gravity to make sure it's within certain limits set by the manufacturer. If it's off-limits you might not be able to recover from a stall, for example, so you shouldn't fly.

Also, if your aircraft weight exceeds the maximum takeoff weight set forth by the manufacturer, you shouldn't fly.

You'll learn that, while all airplanes have published maximum takeoff weights, it doesn't mean you can take off at that weight, any given day, at any airport. If you take off from a high-elevation airport on a hot day, you may not be able to take off unless the aircraft weight is way below the maximum published takeoff weight. Takeoff weight can also be limited by runway length, tyre speed limits, or other reasons.

Many easily avoidable accidents have happened because the pilots failed to calculate a proper weight and balance before a flight. There is no excuse not to calculate weight and balance before a flight. It only takes a couple of minutes to complete after you get the hang of it.

There is a whole weight and balance handbook published by the FAA, downloadable for free from the FAA website or my resources page[14].

It's a good reference book to keep handy, should you move to different aircraft categories. But overall, it's a bit too much information for private pilot studies. Weight and balance computations are usually very simple for small training aircraft. They get more complicated with bigger airplanes, but it's not something you need to worry about at this stage. The most important thing to remember about this subject is that you do the calculations for each flight throughout your whole career, regardless of your aircraft type!

10. Principles of aerodynamics, power plants, and aircraft systems

This can be a very broad subject overall, but it will be broken down into chunks of information that apply to you as a private pilot student.

You will learn the basic aerodynamic principles that apply to all aircraft. This includes what is meant by thrust, drag, lift, and weight in aviation. In addition, you will learn the aerodynamic principles that specifically apply to a single-engine propeller-driven aircraft, such as the left-turning tendencies caused by the propeller and how to counteract them.

The same goes with the power plants and aircraft systems – you will mostly focus on systems that apply to your training aircraft. Therefore, you won't have to spend time learning about jet engines, for example. To prepare for your ground school, it's good to get a copy of the Pilot Operating Handbook (POH) or the Aircraft Flight Manual (AFM) for your training aircraft (send me an email if you don't know where to get one). POH and/or AFM contains information on all the systems installed in your specific training aircraft. It will all feel much less overwhelming if you have some knowledge of your training airplane beforehand!

11. Stall awareness, spin entry, spins, and recovery techniques

Stall and spin awareness is something best learned in the air with your flight instructor, and you will. Still, it's good to first understand the theory behind it. When you first practice stall entries and recoveries in the air, it can be a bit scary. You essentially slow down the aircraft until the wings don't have enough airflow to produce lift to support the aircraft's weight. Once this happens, the aircraft starts to vibrate and shake, which will make it difficult to control; then, it will start to fall from the sky. Scary huh?

Well, it's not really scary at all once you know how to recover from it; and, if you understand the theory behind stalls and spins, you know how to recover from them.

While discussing this topic in ground school, you will learn all the factors affecting an aircraft's stall speeds and why you should always avoid an unintentional stall. You will talk about stalls in different aircraft configurations, such as having the flaps and landing gear up or down or somewhere in-between.

In a spin, the aircraft is spiraling down from the air in a stalled condition. This can happen if the aircraft is first stalled, and one of the wings drops down. Spin training can be a lot of fun, although not all pilots enjoy it. I used to do a lot of spin training in China, and I have a YouTube video[15] (link at the end of the book) to prove it! During private pilot training, you don't have to demonstrate full spin entries and recoveries, but you need to understand how they occur and how to recover from them.

Pilots still enter unintentional stalls and spins occasionally, which is why you will be practicing stall entries and reveries in all kinds of different configurations and circumstances. I still have to demonstrate stall recoveries in a jet aircraft simulator every six or twelve months to keep my type rating current. It's that important.

12. Aeronautical decision making and judgment (ADM)

Nearly eighty percent of all aviation accidents are caused by human error. I don't mean to scare you here. Flying is still extremely safe, but the fact is that accidents still happen. Unfortunately, many of them could have been avoided with proper actions by pilots or other people involved in the causes of the accidents.

Because of these statistics, more and more importance is placed on teaching students aeronautical decision-making (ADM) and exercising good judgment. As a private pilot flying a small aircraft, you will usually be the only pilot aboard. Therefore, your decisions matter because you alone are in charge of flight safety.

It takes time and experience to develop good judgment and decision-making skills in the air. When you are a new pilot, and you can't really judge your own capabilities, it's always better to be on the cautious side. For example, if the weather seems a bit too windy or if it's forecasted to change for the worse before your Estimated Time of Arrival (ETA), it's better to just cancel the flight.

You are likely to go through many case studies about aviation accidents involving good and bad decision-making. One of the grossest examples of bad decision-making is the 2014 Gulfstream IV crash.

The pilots attempted to take off with gust-locks that were locking the flight controls. First, they failed to complete their before start checklist that required the pilot to disengage the gust-locks. Next, they failed to complete the after start checklist, which required them to check the flight control movement. Also, they ignored a "rudder limiter" message that illuminated before take-off. By investigating the cause of the message, they would have realized the gust lock was on. During take-off, they ignored abnormal behavior of the throttles that were limited by the gust locks. During the takeoff roll, after finally realizing the gust lock was on, the captain didn't try to stop the takeoff until eleven seconds later. Sadly, by that time it was too late to stop on the runway.

Everyone on board got killed. Both pilots had many chances to prevent this from happening, by following established procedures that they were trained to follow. This was an easily avoidable accident caused by bad decision-making.

During your training, you will learn about error chains or chains of events that lead to accidents. These chains are used to demonstrate that most accidents are caused by a chain of events. Usually, accidents can be prevented by breaking just one link on the chain. This Gulfstream accident is an example of an error chain where both pilots had many opportunities to avoid the crash by making one right decision. It was an unfortunate and tragic accident, but it makes a good case study for new pilots. It demonstrated the importance of following established procedures and exercising good judgment.

You usually don't hear about the pilots who make good decisions, which includes most pilots every day. Instead, you might hear about a pilot who made a safe landing after declaring an emergency fuel (low fuel situation). Is he a hero? Probably not. Why did he get into the low fuel situation in the first place? Bad planning, perhaps? You might hear about a pilot who landed just seconds before an extremely heavy thunderstorm hit the field. Is he a hero? I don't think so. You shouldn't fly so close to storms. (Been there, done that. By the way, I'm not proud of it.)

Pilots who continuously make good decisions usually have very uneventful flights. They navigate around storms or cumulus clouds to stay safe and comfortable, and they land with plenty of fuel onboard every time.

Sometimes you do hear about pilots who make good

decisions during extreme situations. The "Miracle of Hudson" makes an excellent example of this. The pilots couldn't have predicted hitting that flock of birds before taking off. But when it happened, they did everything right. Instead of panicking and trying to turn back to the airport, they ditched the plane to the Hudson River. Everyone aboard survived. The captain, Chesley "Sully" Sullenberger, wrote a book called *"The Highest Duty: My Search for What Really Matters."*[16] I would definitely recommend you to read it for more in-depth knowledge of a pilot's life.

13. Pre-flight action that includes:

- How to obtain information on runway lengths at airports of intended use; data on takeoff and landing distances; weather reports and forecasts; and fuel requirements.
- How to plan for alternatives if the planned flight cannot be completed or delays are encountered.

This topic basically explains itself. Many of the things concerning pre-flight will be learned before your first flight. Other things, such as planning for alternative airports, you will learn sometime before your cross-country flights. All this is usually covered in a ground school class with other students. Your personal instructor will review the information with you one-on-one before you start flying.

There you go. Now you should have a general idea about the topics you are going to learn in private pilot ground school. Next, let's see how you can prepare before you start your ground school. There are many books you can get for free before you even step into a flight school. So, let me talk about them briefly.

What Books Should I Get to Prepare for Ground School?

Several publishers publish study guides and textbooks to cover all the required knowledge areas for private pilots and other certification levels. But I think the best way for you to get started is to just download all the free FAA publications that cover these areas.

FAA books are official publications that you can use for reference in your practical examinations. The books and/or documents you should study initially include the following:

- Private Pilot Airman Certification Standards
- Pilot's Handbook of Aeronautical Knowledge
- Airplane Flying Handbook
- Aeronautical Information Manual (AIM)
- Federal Aviation Regulations (FAR)
- Aviation Weather Handbook

You can download them all for free from my **resources page** (https://funkypilot.com/resources/), except FAR. Some of them I would also get in paperback for easy reference. Still, first get the electronic copies and decide whether you need the paperback copy later. As for the FARs, you can study them for free online.[17]

Alternatively, you can purchase a paperback or electronic copy of a regulation book that covers all the applicable regulations meant for pilots. An excellent choice for this is the FAR/AIM[18] published by ASA.

You don't have to read any of them cover to cover. Instead, try to get a general idea about the information contained in each book. It will help you with the learning process later.

The first book, *"Private Pilot Airman Certification Standards"* (PPL ACS)[19] is basically a checklist that itemizes all the different knowledge areas, tasks, and skills expected from you by the end of your private pilot training. Reference information found in the ACS points you in the right direction, depending on what knowledge you are studying. Although it may seem a bit confusing, it's mostly just an outline of topics. It's actually an excellent tool that can help you keep track of your progress.

The other books can be quite overwhelming in size, so it's good to use them following your training syllabus rather than reading them all from cover to cover.

As I mentioned, all are free to download. Still, it can be helpful to have physical copies of some of them – especially the FAR/AIM. It's a lovely reference book to have for the whole duration of your training. FAR/AIM combines the applicable Federal Aviation Regulations for pilots and the Aeronautical Information Manual in one neat publication.

Note about Electronic Books and iPads

When I was a student, and when I was instructing, everyone was still using paper books. Currently, electronic books are becoming more and more popular. Depending on your flight school, you may not have to get any paper books, although some schools may still use them.

The FAA handbooks are downloadable in pdf format, so you can read them in just about any device. Some schools, though, may have their own learning apps or software that is only available for specific operating systems.

I had to get an iPad for my EASA studies because I needed a specific flight school app that was only available for iOS. Also, when I do recurrent training for the Bombardier jets that I fly, I need an iPad in the classroom. The training centers usually provide loaner iPads for the week of re-current training. Also my company provides us iPads to use during flying – all our flight manuals and navigational software are loaded in them.

However, even if your school is using electronic books, it's unlikely that that an iPad is included in your training costs. It's good to discus your options with the school before you start your training, you might get by with an Android tablet or a Windows laptop if that's what you prefer.

I find it unfortunate that many aviation apps are not available for other platforms, such as Android or Windows, so in many cases you'll just have to get used to iPads.

Private Pilot Knowledge Examination

To get the private pilot certificate or other FAA certificates covered in this book, you need to take two exams: one knowledge exam and one practical exam. Those are required by the FAA; although, you may have to take additional examinations required by your flight school training program. I will now reference the knowledge exam. The practical test will be explained later.

The FAA PPL knowledge exam is fairly easy. It's often called the written test, although there is no writing involved. It's a computer-based exam with sixty multiple-choice questions. You should answer these within 150 minutes. You need to correctly answer seventy percent or more to pass.

The test includes five questions from each of the following areas of operations:

1. Regulations
2. Accident Reporting
3. Performance Charts
4. Radio Communications
5. Weather
6. Safe and Efficient Operations
7. Density Altitude Performance
8. Weight and Balance

9. Aerodynamics, Powerplants, and Aircraft Systems
10. Stalls and Spins
11. Aeronautical Decision-Making (ADM)
12. Preflight Actions

Seem familiar? Yes, they are the same topics which you will cover in ground school. More than likely, you will cover sample written exam questions during your ground school. It's also likely that you will have to take a practice written exam at the end of your ground course.

If I started to think about becoming a pilot now, I would first begin studying and preparing for the written exam. You only need to be fifteen years old to take the knowledge exam, so you can start preparing early!

Self-Study Courses

During recent years, self-studying has gotten much easier with digital applications that can aid you. Instead of only reading books, you can access excellent videos and graphics with those apps.

There are additional online courses available that have question banks of similar questions you can expect to see on the exam. You need to make sure you understand all the material, but when you study those questions and answers, you are practically guaranteed to pass the test with a high score.

Companies and organizations such as Aircraft Owners and Pilots Association (AOPA),[20] Gleim,[21] and Sporty's[22] offer lots of free material for PPL students. Paid courses are offered for more advanced training. You can find links to some of the recommended applications and study courses from my resources page.

Endorsement Needed for Knowledge Exam

One more thing about the knowledge examination: You will need an endorsement from an authorized instructor stating that you are ready for the exam. To get the endorsement, you don't necessarily need to set your foot into a flight school. You don't even need to meet with an instructor to get the endorsement. The online preparation courses I mentioned offer you with the required endorsement after you have completed all the required exercises.

Upon having the endorsement, you can schedule yourself to take the exam. If you are studying in 141 schools, the ground instructor will help you schedule it. If you are studying on your own, you can easily schedule it by yourself by contacting one of the testing centers.

FAA Testing Centers

The FAA maintains a website with testing recourses for pilots[23]. From there you will be directed to another website that will help you locate a testing center[24] — and to schedule your exam when you are ready. There are hundreds of testing centers; nearly a thousand in fact. So, it's very likely that you live nearby one.

The testing centers are usually located in dedicated areas inside some flight schools. Even your flight school may be a dedicated testing center, which would be very convenient for you.

The testing rooms are usually small rooms with just a few computers. There will be video surveillance to prevent cheating, because there is no room for cheating in aviation anyway. Cheating could endanger flight safety, so don't even think about it.

Taking the Test

A proctor will give you instructions on how to start the test, what equipment you are allowed to use during the test, what do to in case you need to use the bathroom, etc. There is nothing complicated about it. Once you start the test, relax. Take your time to read each question carefully before answering, and pick an answer.

If you don't know some answers, you can flag questions and review them after you answer all the other questions. Even if you choose an answer to each question, you can review the exam before submitting the answers. One hundred fifty minutes is plenty of time to review each question several times if necessary. Still, I'm sure you will complete the exam long before the time is up!

For more information that will help you prepare for the PPL written test, you should also take a look at the Private Pilot Knowledge Test Guide[25] and Appendixes one, two, three, located in the Private Pilot Airman Certification Standards (PPL ACS).

Next, let's talk about flight training.

Flight Training and Flight Time Requirements

Under Part 61, you are required to log at least forty flight hours. This should include at least ten hours of "solo" flight, and twenty hours "dual" flight training provided by an authorized instructor.

Dual flight training means you fly with an authorized instructor. Solo training means you fly alone, and there is nobody else in the aircraft.

In Part 141 schools, the total flight hour requirement is thirty-five hours. This should include five hours solo flight and twenty hours with an instructor. The remaining ten hours can be used in whatever way is required by your 141 training syllabus.

Most students need more than forty hours of training to gain the necessary skills needed to pass the PPL practical exam, regardless of the flight school. While it's good to aim for the minimum hours, don't worry if you need a few extra hours. The extra hours usually count towards your total time for a commercial license later on. So, it's all useful experience.

Some of the training requirements vary based on the category and class of aircraft you use. In this context, an aircraft category has a broad meaning. It includes the airplane, rotorcraft, glider, and lighter-than-air. Aircraft class refers to single-engine land or sea, multi-engine land or sea, gyro-plane, helicopter, airship, and free balloon.

These are some of the terms that are defined in 14 CFR Part 1 — Definitions and Abbreviations.[26] You will normally talk about them in your first ground lesson, which is about regulations; so it's good if you already understand their meaning.

I will only cover the training requirements for single-engine airplane training, which is the most common type of aircraft for private pilot training.

Your flight training will cover the following areas of operations:

1. Pre-flight preparation
2. Pre-flight procedures
3. Airport operations
4. Takeoffs, landings, and go-arounds
5. Performance maneuvers
6. Ground reference maneuvers
7. Navigation
8. Slow flight and stalls
9. Basic instrument maneuvers
10. Emergency operations
11. Night operations (optional in some cases, but required for pilots who plan to fly at night)
12. Post-flight procedures

The requirements for the skills you need to learn for each area of operation are listed in the PPL ACS. Again, it's a good document to use as a checklist, thereby making sure you cover each required maneuver or skill during your training.

Also, it's a good reference book that reminds you about the required standards for each task or skill you need to learn. For example, if you go to page thirty-four in the PPL ACS. You can see that for steep turns you need to maintain the entry altitude +/- 100 feet, airspeed +/- 10 knots, and so on. Each maneuver has specific standards you need to meet by the end of the private pilot training course. The standards usually involve maintaining headings, altitudes, and speeds within certain criteria.

Furthermore, your **dual** flight training needs to include at least:

- Three hours of cross-country flight training in a single-engine airplane.
- Three hours of night flight training.
- Three hours of flight training solely by the reference to instruments.
- Three hours of flight training in preparation for the practical test within sixty days preceding the date of the test.

Your **solo** flights need to include at least:

- Ten hours of solo flight time in certain areas of operation if you train in 61 schools.
- Five hours of solo flight time in certain areas of operation if you train in 141 schools.
- One solo cross-country flight with landings at a minimum of three points. One of the segments has to be more than fifty nautical miles of straight-line distance. The total distance should be at least a hundred nautical miles under 141 rules and 150 nautical miles under 61 rules.
- Three takeoffs and landings at an airport with an operating control tower. (If you train at an uncontrolled airfield such as I did, then you can meet this requirement during your cross-country flights to controlled airports).
- Five hours of solo cross-country time if you train in a part 61 school.

The cross-country distance requirements may vary if you live on small islands or in Hawaii (due to the lack of proper airports). The night flight requirements may vary if you live in Alaska (where the sun may not set at times). You can find the exact requirements in 14 CFR Part 61, but I'm sure your flight instructor will explain if there are any special requirements or omissions regarding your training.

All this may seem a lot, but it's actually not that much when approaching it in a step-by-step manner. It took me slightly over fifty hours of training and over two months to get my private pilot license. But when I became an instructor, I was working in flight schools that offered accelerate training. Just about all the students got their private pilot licenses in a month or less, and with minimum hours.

I trained probably a hundred students that way, and none of them failed a single practical exam! The students were required to fly almost every day – once, twice, or even three times a day. And, it worked. Then again, I don't know if this type of method would have worked for me. I was still struggling with understanding aviation English when I was a student. By reading this book, you are already in a better position for more efficient training than I ever was!

My point is that I think it's good to get your private pilot certificate as quickly as possible. It will significantly increase your confidence level. You can call yourself a pilot once you finish, and you'll be hooked on aviation for life!

But you should also know your limits. Accelerated training won't work for you unless you are properly prepared for each lesson, and have done most of your ground school studies in advance.

If your flight training follows the accelerated method, meaning you fly twice or more per day, then you should definitely complete your ground school studies and the knowledge exam before starting to fly. You wouldn't want to finish all your flight training, and then having to spend time finishing the ground school and the written exam. That's because you can't complete your practical exam until you have taken the written exam. It's in your best interest to take the practical exam as soon as possible after your last flight lesson.

Private Pilot Training Progression

Regardless of the flight school at which you train, your training is going to follow a certain outline. You are going to start with simple tasks, moving onto more difficult ones. It's called a building block approach to flight training. You build on previously learned knowledge and skills.

In general, private pilot flight training is divided into three stages, followed by a practical examination:

- **Stage One** — Pre-solo Stage

- **Stage Two** — Cross-Country and Night Flight Stage
- **Stage Three** — Solo Cross-Country and Flight Review Stage
- **Practical Examination**

Next, I will briefly describe each flight training stage.

I won't discuss all the procedures and maneuvers in-depth because they are better learned with graphical presentations. Moreover, it's outside the scope of this book to include graphics. However, the Airplane Flying Handbook,[27] a free download, explains all the maneuvers in detail. It has excellent pictures to help you. Just look at the book's table of contents and find the maneuvers you want to study.

Stage 1 — Pre-Solo Stage

The goal of the pre-solo stage is for you to get familiar with the training airplane, and gaining enough experience to operate it safely by yourself on a solo flight.

Wow! It sounds like an important stage! Yes, pre-solo stage is probably the most important stage in your whole training. Once you complete this stage, you can do your first solo flight. It validates that you can fly an airplane without any supervision!

After the first solo, you can be confident that you can become a pilot. And, you will know you are not wasting your time and money with the training.

Although this is a very important stage, it's not as long and difficult as you might think. The training airplanes for private pilot training are not very complex. Depending on your training schedule, you could complete the pre-solo stage in a week or two. But of course, it would take longer if you have many days off between your flights.

It usually takes about ten to twenty hours of flight training before your first solo. More if you have long gaps between your training flights, or if you don't properly prepare for the lessons. Based on my experience, at this stage, shorter flight lessons prepare students faster for solo flights. By shorter, I mean one-hour lessons seem to be better than one and a half hours or two-hour lessons.

You are more likely to fly solo after fifteen hours if you do fifteen one-hour flights instead of ten one and a half hours flight lessons. That's because, after about an hour, you are likely to start getting tired. It gets hard to focus on practicing the same things over and over if you spend two hours training all different maneuvers.; your lesson wouldn't be focused enough to improve certain aspects of your flight skills.

That's something you should discuss with your instructor before you even start taking your lessons. But don't worry about it too much if the lessons in your syllabus are one and a half- or two-hour lessons. They probably have a good reason for it, depending on the airport and airspace where you train. Also, the times are usually just recommendations. If you talk to your instructor, you can probably keep the lessons shorter.

Watch out for instructors who like to keep the lessons long, loitering around the training area – they may be just after the flight hours or the pay it brings them, instead of teaching you. Always remember, you are the customer who is paying for training.

What to Expect in This Stage:

Pre-flight Procedures

An instructor will show you different preflight procedures before your first flight. Pre-flight procedures include things such as: checking the weather forecast for your flight; filing a flight plan if necessary; estimating how much fuel you will need; calculating the weight and balance for the aircraft; and/or discussing what you are going to do during the flight.

Pre-flight Briefing

Before each flight you should also do a "pre-flight briefing" with you instructor. During the briefing you will review your pre-flight planning and you will discuss what you are going to do during the flight lesson. Pre-flight briefings help you prepare for the task ahead, and the set the tone for the operation, establish expectations, and inform you (the student) of things to come.

Pre-flighting the Airplane

You will also learn how to 'pre-flight' the airplane. By 'pre-flighting,' I mean conducting a pre-flight inspection of the airplane. You will need to visually inspect and determine that the aircraft is in a safe condition for a flight. This process is also known as a "walkaround." Your instructor will guide you through the process, explaining what to check and how to check items on the aircraft. In general, you will visually check that all the aircraft's different parts are in good condition. Check the fuel and oil levels, and that all required documents are up-to-date and aboard. Remove different tie-downs and protective covers, checking that no screws are loose or missing from the airframe. Check that the tires don't have flat spots, and that the hydraulic breaks are not leaking, etc.

The pre-flight is usually a whole ground lesson in itself. It takes quite some time when you first do it. First few times, though, you will pre-flight the aircraft together with your instructor until you are familiar with the process. Later on, you will be doing it by yourself before your instructor arrives at the aircraft.

Ground Operations

On the ground, you will become familiar with the engine start procedures, taxiing the aircraft, and running through different checklists.

Your instructor will guide you on how to accomplish each required task by using different checklists. There is a checklist full of items for each phase of a flight. For example, on the ground, you normally have to run through a pre-flight checklist, before-start checklist, after-start checklist, taxi checklist, and a before-takeoff checklist. In the air you run through a bunch of other checklists.

Once you get the engine started and run through all

the after start checks, you'll get your first experience with ATC. Your instructor will most likely do all the radio calls on your first flight, but it's good for you to listen. Try to understand what is being said.

Before you can taxi (taxiing means driving the airplane on the ground), you will need permission from the ground control. That is if you train at a controlled airport. If you train at an uncontrolled airport, you don't need permission to taxi. Instead, you would simply announce your intentions to taxi on a common traffic advisory frequency of your airport.

Taxiing

Taxiing the aircraft for the first time can feel strange. That's because you are not steering the aircraft by using your hands. Instead, you will have to use your feet. If you are used to driving cars or bikes, your natural instinct will be to grab the control wheel (or stick, depending on your aircraft type), that's in front of you and use it for steering. But, the control column won't help you steer the aircraft on the ground. It only turns the ailerons in the wings and has little effect on steering on the ground.

To turn the aircraft on the ground, you will have to press pedals with your feet. The pedals are connected to the rudder and, in most airplanes, to the nose wheel. Together the rudder and the nose wheel steering system help you turn the aircraft on the ground. The pedals have a second function — braking. Pushing the tops of the pedals with your toes activates the wheel brakes. Differential braking can be used to assist steering on the ground especially for tight turns. Some airplane models don't even have a nose wheel steering system, in which case you would use differential breaking more frequently during turns.

While you use your feet for steering, your right hand should be on the throttle lever that controls the engine speed. You will be sitting on the left seat while your instructor sits on the right seat. The throttle lever is somewhere in the middle, depending on your aircraft type. When you push the throttle forward, the aircraft will accelerate and decelerate when you pull it back.

Your left hand should be on the control wheel or a stick, so that you can adjust the aileron positions based on the wind direction. You will learn about cross-wind taxi techniques or how to position the ailerons during taxiing in windy conditions from your instructor.

Also, while you are taxiing, you need to pay attention to airport signs, other airplanes, and your wingtips. Make sure you don't hit anything. Most of your attention should be on the outside of the aircraft.

It takes some time to grasp the idea of steering with your feet and controlling the speed with your hand. But after a few flights, it usually becomes second nature to most students. Taxiing is not something to stress about. You'll be surprised how quickly you will get comfortable operating the aircraft on the ground.

Your First Flight

Your first flight is usually a short introductory lesson on how to operate the aircraft on the ground and in the air.

In the air, you will fly to some predetermined training area near the airport. Here your instructor will teach you how to establish different flight attitudes such as straight and level flight, turns, climbs, and descents.

These are very basic maneuvers, but it can still be quite an overwhelming experience for the first time. So many dials and gauges moving in the instrument panel! So many things to see outside! But the idea is to get familiar with the aircraft controls and get a feeling of three-dimensional flight.

At first, you don't even have to worry too much about the instruments inside the cockpit. Most likely, your instructor will encourage you to keep looking outside instead. You should observe the location of the horizon when you do different maneuvers. It's all about visual flying in the private pilot stage. You'll be focusing on the flight instruments later.

You will also learn to run through checklist items in the air. These checklists normally include an after takeoff checklist, climb checklist, cruise checklist, descent checklist, and approach checklist. The checklists' names and included items vary between aircraft types. Just be prepared to follow them and don't skip any items.

Once you learn how to do basic turns, climbs, and descents, you will learn more and more new and advanced maneuvers during the following flights.

Post-flight Briefing

Back on the ground, you will do a post-flight briefing (or debriefing). During post-flight briefing you will discuss your experiences during the flight. You will talk about what you did good or what didn't go so well. It's important to do a post-flight briefing after each flight so you can analyze any failures and improve your performance on the next flight.

Briefings and debriefings makes successful competition of the present flight, and future flights, more likely, so don't get frustrated if you need to spend some time in the briefing room after each flight!

Pre-Solo Flight Training

After the first flight, you will gradually be introduced to new maneuvers. You will also review previously learned ones. Maneuvers that you will learn in this stage include: steep turns, slow flight, and stall recoveries.

You will further learn ground reference maneuvers. These are turns around a point and s-turns across a road and rectangular course. All these maneuvers are designed to teach you to safely control the aircraft while dividing your attention between inside and outside references.

All these maneuvers additionally prepare you for flying the airplane in the airport traffic pattern. Airport traffic patterns are developed to ensure safe traffic flow into and outside of an airport. The direction of the traffic flow, the placement, and the height of the pattern vary based on the local conditions of each airport.

In the traffic pattern (also known as a circuit), you will need to know how to slow down the aircraft. This is why you practice slow flight in the practice area first. You will need to be able to recover from an inadvertent stall in case you slow down too much, and that's why you practice stall recoveries. The ground reference maneuvers are practiced, so that you can fly a rectangular traffic pattern around the airport without being pushed away by the wind.

Basic Instrument Flying

In the training area, you will also be introduced to flying solely by the reference of flight instruments. You will simulate instrument flying by wearing some type of a view limiting device designed for this purpose. This training is important. It will help you remain oriented in case you accidentally end up in clouds during your solo flights later.

Takeoffs and Landings

Takeoffs and landings are the most critical phases of flight because you operate close to the ground. While during the first few flights you will focus on training individual maneuvers, you will also get familiar with takeoffs and landings. Every flight involves at least one takeoff and one landing, which is another reason shorter flights initially can help get you ready for solo flights faster.

After a few flights in a training area, you will spend several flights in the airport traffic pattern. You will practice: normal takeoffs and landings; crosswind takeoffs and landings; go-arounds from rejected landings; no flap landings; forward slips to landings; and emergency approaches to landings. You will also learn about different system malfunctions that can happen during flight, so that you will be prepared for all kinds of situations.

That's quite a few things to discuss and practice in the traffic pattern alone. It will be exciting and satisfying when you make your first few landings without the instructor helping with the controls.

All this sounds a lot, but after a while, it all becomes second nature. Once your instructor determines you are ready for a solo flight, you will have your first stage check — if it's required by your training curriculum. Stage checks are a normal part of 141 training, but you may not have to do them in 61 schools.

Pre-Solo Stage Check

A stage check is a flight you will do with a flight instructor, other than the one who is training you. You will have to demonstrate that you possess all the required skills and knowledge to move onto the next stage. There might also be an oral portion to the check, in which the check instructor can ask questions relating to the stage of training.

In 141 schools, you are usually required to do three different stage checks during your private pilot training. Stage checks are not required from 61 schools, but some schools may conduct them anyway. If your school doesn't require them, it would be up to you and your instructor to determine when you are ready for a solo flight.

The purpose of a stage check is to simply get a second opinion or validation of your progress. Stage checks can be beneficial in discovering any shortcomings in your training. Your instructor may have unintentionally overlooked some aspects of the curriculum.

In the pre-solo stage check, the instructor mostly wants to see you can safely takeoff and land with the aircraft, as well as do the required maneuvers up to certain standards. In the check's oral portion, the check instructor would want to make sure you understand all the rules and procedures. After all, you would have to follow these during a solo flight.

If your instructor thinks you are ready for a solo flight, then you shouldn't have any problems passing the stage check. However, if for some reason you fail the check, don't worry about it. It doesn't mean you can't become a pilot. It just means you'll need a bit of extra training before moving onto the next stage of training. Usually, one or two extra flights will fix whatever needs fixing. Then, you can keep moving on with your training. No big deal.

Your First Solo (and mine)

"Do not let yourself be forced into doing anything before you are ready."
— *Wilbur Wright*

Your first solo flight will be the flight you'll probably remember forever. It's the last flight of the first stage of training. This is the first first time you will be alone in the cockpit. There will be nobody in the backseat, even if your aircraft has one. At this point, you have already done many takeoffs and landings under your instructor's supervision. But on your last couple of flights, your instructor did not give you any assistance with the controls — he (or she) was only a passenger. Now it's time to do the same, only without a passenger.

The first solo flight is actually a 'supervised solo.' Your instructor needs to be at the airport supervising the flight from the ground while you are flying. The flight is conducted in two parts: first, a dual flight, which is immediately followed by a solo flight.

If the airport has a control tower, you and/or your instructor may notify the controllers about your first solo. This way, the air traffic controllers will make sure to give you enough space in the pattern. Some airports can get busy with five or more small planes practicing landings at the same time. But normally, first solos are done early in the morning or just before sunset when the airport is not too busy. This is also when the air is usually less turbulent.

In 2000, I did my first solo flight with a small Cessna 152 aircraft in Conway, South Carolina. It was a nice April evening, about an hour before sunset. I had successfully completed my pre-solo stage check the day before. The nice thing about flying in the evening was that almost everyone else at the school had gone home. So, I had the traffic pattern for myself.

During the first part of the flight mission, I completed two takeoffs and landings with my instructor. This was the last check to validate my flight skills. My instructor didn't have to give me any instructions or touch the controls during the flight. So, she determined that I was ready for the solo.

It was also my last chance to decide if I was ready.

As Wilbur Wright said: *"Do not let yourself be forced into doing anything before you are ready."* It's important that you are also confident and ready to do the flight. In my case, I was ready.

After the two landings together, we taxied back to the ramp, and my instructor signed a solo endorsement in the back of my flight logbook. We shut down the engine, and she got out of the airplane. Once she was a safe distance away, I started the engine again for the second part of the flight. Many instructors leave the plane with the engine running while the student stays in the plane, but some schools prohibit such practice for safety reasons.

Next, I taxied back to the runway of the uncontrolled airport, announced my intentions via the radio, and took off...

It was exciting to fly an airplane alone for the first time! Nervous, thrilled, excited, happy, amazed, proud, surprised — You pick the adjective! So many feelings all at once!

It was all up to me now. I was put off-guard by how fast the small plane climbed with only one person aboard. I was up at the 1000-foot traffic pattern altitude in no time. After leveling off, it was such a peaceful feeling listening to the humming of the aircraft with nobody else around. Yet, looking down at the airport made me nervous because I had to somehow return there. When I was making my way back for a landing, it felt amazing considering how little power was required to maintain level flight. And, it was remarkable how much throttle I had to reduce to descent at normal rate for landing.

I completed the first circuit and made a full-stop landing. After landing, I exited the runway and taxied back to the takeoff end of the runway. I was not allowed to do touch-and-goes on the first solo. I had to make full-stop landings, taxi back to the beginning of the runway, and take off again. I completed a total of five takeoffs and landings this way, and the whole thing took me exactly one hour.

After I parked and shut down the aircraft, my fellow student pilots came to grab me from the airplane. They carried me out to a little grassy area in front of the school and dropped me into a ditch that was filled with water! Actually, it was barely a ditch at all, so they also threw some buckets of water at me! That was a traditional ditching ceremony which happens to many student pilots after their first solo! Don't know who started it and when, but it happens in many flight schools, at least in the United States.

This was my first solo experience. I believe yours will be similar, except you may only have to do one, two, or three takeoffs and landings instead of five. And, there may not be ditching involved at the end of the flight. But who cares about the minor details? The main thing is to get it done. Be proud of yourself. Perhaps take the night off from your aeronautical studies and celebrate!

Stage Two — Cross Country / Night Flight Stage

This is a kinda fun stage. You will finally learn how to fly from one airport to another, which is the main reason for air transportation.

In the second stage of your training, you will learn to navigate to different airports away from your local airport. Flying from one airport to another is called cross-country flying. For training purposes, the airports have to be located at least 50 nautical miles apart. You will need at least three hours of cross-country training to get your private pilot certificate.

It takes a lot of preparation to leave your home base. You will learn to fill navigation logs, check airport information, check the weather for the route, calculate takeoff and landing distances, plan for fuel burn, read the paper navigational charts (yes, paper charts are still used), etc. You will also be introduced to diversion and planning of alternative airports, as well as lost procedures.

In this stage, you will usually learn how to do short-

and soft-field takeoffs and landings. You might be flying to different airports that have shorter fields to which you are accustomed, or you might even fly to grass fields. So, this is a good time to learn these techniques. Other than that, there shouldn't be any other new maneuvers introduced at this stage.

In order for you to gain night flight privileges, you will further do night flight training at this stage.

And of course, throughout your training, you will keep reviewing previously learned maneuvers to constantly improve your skills and flight techniques. Between dual flights, you normally do more solo flights to the local training areas or the traffic pattern to gain more experience as the pilot in command.

Cross-Country Navigation

During the cross-country flights, you will learn to navigate using pilotage, dead reckoning, electronic navigational aids, or other forms of navigational means.

Navigating with modern airplanes using electronic navigational means is easy. You already know about GPS satellites traveling in orbit, right? You simply program your route to the GPS receiver and follow the directions. Easy. But you will also learn about some ground-based navigational aids such as VOR and NDB.

They are also quite simple to use after you study how they work.

But the main focus of private pilot navigation training will be in pilotage and dead reckoning. You are expected to keep looking outside and follow visual ground references.

Pilotage is basically navigation by ground, referencing points that you select from a sectional chart (a map for visual flying) before the flight. Dead reckoning is navigation by means of computations based on time, speed, distance, headings, and weather conditions. These two methods are used together during your cross-country flights. You will be tested on them during the practical exam, so try to resist the urge just to follow the GPS.

You will practice all these methods during your cross-country flights. During the flights, you will have to use paper or electronic maps, and you will need to fill a navigational log with times and fuel burn over each checkpoint.

It's all quite easy training. And, it's usually more enjoyable than practicing those endless stalls, steep turns, and other maneuvers. Cross-country flying is what flying is all about — going from one place to another. This stage will highly improve your situational awareness because you will pay more attention to which way you are going. Also, you will learn to contact different ATC facilities along the way.

The navigation part can be very easy or a bit challenging, depending on the location where you fly. I used to fly a lot in Florida. Many of the airports there are located near the coast, so navigating was easy by just following the coastline. But when flying to airports located more inland, such as Gainesville or Orlando, things were a bit more difficult. There were not that many easily recognizable ground references on the way.

It can be easy to get lost in the air if you don't have good checkpoints in the area. But no worries — you will also learn about lost procedures in this stage. You will learn how to contact the ATC for help, how to find your location by electrical means, and how to visually determine your location based on outside references.

Most airports with flight schools are located in areas where there is radar coverage from ATC. And if you are flying in a radar coverage area, you can always contact the ATC. They will be happy to give you directions to the nearest airport whenever needed. ATC is there to help you.

Checking the weather forecasts is an important step in preparation for any flight. But the weather can change fast, and forecasts are not always correct. If you can't continue to your destination airport due to bad weather or for some other reason, you will have to divert to another airport.

Diversion to another airport is something you will also practice in this stage. At some point during a training flight, your instructor will ask you to divert to some nearby airport. You will have to calculate your required heading, time, distance, and fuel burn to reach the airport. You will do all this while you are flying the aircraft. And, I doubt your training airplane has an autopilot to help you while you do your calculations!

Overall, it can be a lot of fun flying to different airports. Even better if you can keep the plane for the whole day and stop for lunch somewhere. I used to do many cross-country flights with my students from Orlando to Venice Beach, Florida. After arriving in Venice Beach, we would have lunch at a beach restaurant nearby! Great way to spend a day!

Night Flying

You are required to do at least three hours of night flight training during your PPL course. The three hours should include at least ten takeoffs and ten landings to a full-stop at an airport. Yep, it needs to be at an airport like the regulations say. Don't go landing in some random field or a ditch! You will also need to do one nighttime cross-country flight that is over a hundred nautical miles in total distance.

While it's called night flying, it doesn't mean you have to do the flights very late at night. Nighttime starts one hour after the sunset, which, of course, varies based on your location and time of the year.

Night flying is usually very pleasant. The cooler air provides a smoother flight experience, and usually, there is a lot less other air traffic around. During the night flights (or hopefully before), you will learn about different visual illusions pilots can experience at night. It's easy to get disoriented while flying at night because there might not be a clear horizon you would normally use as a visual reference for your attitude.

You will learn to understand why it's important to trust the instruments regardless of what your physical feelings are telling you. During night flight training, you will also learn the importance and meaning of the different lights in the aircraft and around the airport.

There are no solo night flights required until your commercial pilot training.

Stage-Two Check

Normally there is a stage-two check that you have to complete before you are allowed to do solo cross-country flights. But again, it depends on your flight training curriculum.

In your second-stage check, you will be tested on navigation by pilotage, dead reckoning, and by other means available to you. You will also have to know how to divert to an alternative airport and what to do in case you get lost. Usually, at the end of the check, you will also do a couple of short- and soft-field takeoffs and landings. These prove that you can land on different types of runways if necessary.

The main focus of the test is to see that you can safely fly to different airports without getting lost. But depending on the curriculum, you may also be tested on some other maneuvers you learned during the stage, as well as on different emergency procedures of the aircraft in which you are flying.

Final Stage — Solo Cross-Country Flights and Flight Review

The last stage in your private pilot training is usually very quick. At this point, you have already learned all the maneuvers and skills required by private pilot applicants. You will just have to complete your solo cross-country requirements and review everything you have learned.

Solo Cross-Country Flights

The solo cross-country requirements differ slightly in 61 and 141 schools. But in either case, you will need another logbook endorsement from your instructor for the solo cross-country flights. Your previous solo endorsement was only for local flights. Solo cross-country flights require a different endorsement, and you can't fly solo to other airports without it.

If you train in a 61 school, you need to log at least five hours of solo cross-country time. In 141 schools, there are no specific time requirements.

Under both rules, you are required to complete one cross-country flight that has landings at a minimum of three points. It has one flight segment with a straight line distance of more than fifty nautical miles. The total distance of this flight differs, however. Under 61 rules, the total distance has to be at least 150 nautical miles, while under 141 rules it needs only to be a hundred nautical miles.

In addition, during your solo cross-country flights, you need to do three takeoffs and three landings at an airport with an operating control tower. You can meet this requirement during your three-point cross-country flight, or you can do an additional cross-country flight if necessary.

Because I did my training in a 141 school, I didn't have any time requirements. During my PPL training, I did one long cross-country flight that took me four hours. I did takeoffs and landings in four different airports. Because my school was located at an uncontrolled airport without a control tower, I had to do three land-ings in three other airports. This is why I had to make a four-point cross-country flight instead of a three-point.

Flight Review and Final Stage Check

After you finish your solo cross-country flight(s), you are near the end of your private pilot training. At this point, you should have mastered all the required maneu-vers and met all the flight training requirements.

Now, it's time to review everything and identify if anything needs improvement. By now, you probably know if you struggle to maintain altitude with steep turns or loose your heading during stall recovery. No worries, because this is the time to keep practicing those maneuvers until you meet the standards required by the private pilot certification standards.

Once you and your instructor determine you are ready for the practical examination, you will do your final stage check. Or, if your curriculum doesn't require stage checks, your instructor can schedule you for the practical examination straight away.

The final stage check is like a simulated practical exam. You will need to do all the maneuvers up to the PPL standards. During the oral portion of the check, an instructor may ask you the same questions which you can expect during the actual test.

If everything goes well, then you can proceed and move onto the private pilot practical exam. But if the check instructor is not happy with your performance, then you may have to review some items with your instructor and then try again.

I only did two flights between my second and third stage checks. Those were my one solo cross-country flight and one review flight with my instructor. After the review, I did the final stage check, and after that, I did the practical exam with an FAA examiner.

So, in my case, the final stage was barely a stage at all. Basically, I just had to finish my solo cross country requirements. At this point, I was ready for the checkride. In your school, the stages may be organized a bit differently, but the result will be the same. You just need to make sure you meet all the aeronautical experience and knowledge requirements set forth by the private pilot airman certification standards before the practical exam.

Private Pilot Practical Examination

After you have completed all your flight and ground training requirements, it's time for the practical examination. In the United States, the practical exam is more commonly called a "checkride." Elsewhere it may be called the "skills test."

The practical examination is the last step in obtaining any pilot certificate. It will consist of two parts — the oral exam and flight exam.

You will need another logbook endorsement from your instructor to take the exam. The endorsement is valid for sixty days, and unless you complete your checkride within that time, you will have to do three hours of flight review before you can get a new endorsement.

Your instructor will help you schedule the practical examination, and it's usually best to schedule it as early as possible after you are ready. Don't go traveling or vacationing after your final stage check. Keep the momentum flowing and take the checkride the next day, if possible.

It can be beneficial to you if your instructor knows the examiner personally or has previously sent other students to the particular examiner. Your instructor might be able to tell you what to expect from the examiner, so that you can focus your last minute studies more appropriately.

It's natural to be nervous before and during a checkride. Although, there is no reason to doubt yourself if you completed all your training and your instructor is confident enough to sign you off for a checkride! You are ready, and you can do it!

Many pilots actually feel the final stage check is more difficult than the actual checkride since they usually cover every possible scenario in the final stage check. The actual checkride may not be so thorough because the examiner doesn't have to test you on everything. Instead, he can choose some tasks on each area of operation that need to be tested.

Your flight instructor and the flight school have the responsibility of only signing off students who are absolutely ready for the practical exams. The FAA examiner conducting the checkride knows this, and so they usually go easier on you. They know you have been validated by your instructor and a possible check instructor already.

Before you go to your checkride, you should complete a Practical Test Checklist that you can find from Appendix page A-11 in the PPL ACS. It's just a list of items you should bring with you to the test. Make sure you have everything prepared at least a day before the check.

Also, make sure you read through Appendix 5: Practical Test Roles, Responsibilities, and Outcomes of the ACS. It will help you better understand what to expect from the test.

Oral Exam

For most people, the oral exam is the tough part of the checkride. The flying part is usually easy because, after enough training, flight skills become part of your physical memory. You won't have to think about the flight maneuvers much. At this point, everything should already feel natural.

The oral exam is different. You may not be used to talking about different areas of aviation to an unknown person, and things may feel difficult to explain. In the oral exam, you will sit down with an FAA examiner. He/she will ask you different questions about all areas of required aviation knowledge.

If the examiner determines you have sufficient knowledge to be a private pilot, you will move onto the flying part. But if you can't answer to his questions correctly, you may have to discontinue the checkride.

You may wonder what is the examiner going to ask.

You may start to worry that, even after you have studied all the textbooks and manuals, you can't remember everything. There is so much material. How could you remember everything? It sounds kind of horrifying to be grilled about aviation knowledge like that, doesn't it?

These are common thoughts. It's natural to be nervous and stressed before a checkride. But first of all, you don't need to remember every little detail you have studied in the books. Of course, you need to have good knowledge of safety operations and rules of the air. However, you won't have to explain every little detail of your aircraft's electrical system for example. Or you won't have to go in too much detail about different weather patterns. The questions are normally fairly simple, at least on the private pilot level. Moreover, there are some good ways to prepare yourself.

To prepare for the practical exam, I would recommend you download the *"Private Pilot Airman Certification Standards."* Use it as your checklist. Everything that you are expected to do or be able to explain is listed there.

For example: Page three of the ACS shows the first area of operation that is 'Pre-flight Preparation.' There is a table that shows Task A is 'Pilot Qualifications.' Next, you can see the 'References' for this task. It's a list of FAA books or manuals where you can find all the required information for this task. That will tell you exactly where to go to refresh your memory. There is a list of items that you (the applicant) need to know – "The applicant demonstrates understanding of:"

- Requirements for certification, recent flight experience, and record keeping.
- Privileges and limitations.
- Medical certificates: class, expirations, privileges, temporary disqualifications.
- Documents required to exercise private pilot limitations.
- Part 68 BasicMed privileges and limitations.

Those are the areas in this task about which the examiner may ask you questions. After studying these areas, you would move on to the next task, and so on.

If you systematically study each knowledge area, you will be well-prepared for your checkride. Don't worry about remembering everything, but make sure you know where to find the information. If you don't remember something, the examiner will usually let you find the information from your books.

During your training, you probably learn things in a different order. But I think following this 'checklist' while preparing yourself for the checkride can be very helpful, since you can keep track of your progress.

There are some guides that can also be very useful in preparing for your oral exam. The Oral Exam guides, published by ASA, follow the same task by task way of presenting things as the ACS.

The oral exam guides only give you very short answers to each question. I wouldn't recommend you use them as your sole source for studying. However, I think they can be very useful in refreshing your memory before the checkride. Use this resource when you only have limited time for preparation. You can find links to the oral exam guides from my flight training page (https://funkypilot.com/aviation/flight-training/).[28]

Once you complete the oral part of the examination, you will move onto the flight part. It's usually done right away after the oral exam, just as long as the weather is good.

However, if the examiner finds your aviation knowledge unsatisfactory, you may have to discontinue the test. In this case you would have to review with your instructor the knowledge area(s) that you were weak on, and then re-schedule the test.

This is not a good feeling, but it's really no big deal. The second time around is usually very quick. Normally you would just have to explain the things you didn't know, or couldn't remember, the first time around.

I have failed one of my oral exams during my career, and the re-take only took about two minutes. The examiner just wanted to hear the answer to one question I couldn't answer on the first try. Once I correctly answered the question, we moved on to the flying part. No big deal.

Flight Examination

The flying part normally starts by you flying out from the airport, following a cross-country plan toward a pre-determined airport. After you reach your first or second cross-country checkpoint, the examiner will usually ask you to divert somewhere else. You need to demonstrate that you won't get lost if you can't continue to your destination.

Next, you will do some (or all) of the maneuvers which you practiced during your training: steep turns, slow flight, stalls, emergency descent, and some ground reference maneuvers. If everything goes well, you will return to the airport and do some takeoffs and landings. You will have to demonstrate normal, short-field, and soft-field takeoffs and landings, as well as a go-around.

You should be okay, just as long as the examiner

doesn't have to take controls or doesn't have to teach you how to do things. The flight is like any other training flight, except that the examiner is there only to observe you. He might give you some pointers about how to improve your skills, but mostly he should simply observe and tell you what to do next.

If, for some reason, you can't perform the maneuvers up to the PPL standards, the examiner may have to fail you. If this happens, again no big deal. You'll just have to do a review flight(s) with your instructor to practice the maneuvers you were weak on, and then re-schedule the test.

In the re-test you would normally only do the maneuver(s) you failed on, meaning the flight will probably be very short. You won't have to re-do all the maneuvers you already successfully demonstrated.

The flying part of my private pilot checkride only took me 1.2 hours (one hour and twelve minutes). Easy flight.

Once you finish the flight part of the checkride, there will still be a post-flight briefing. You will fill your logbook, while the examiner prints and signs a temporary private pilot certificate. The temporary certificate is valid for 120 days. You should get the actual credit-card-looking certificate by mail within that time.

Congratulations! You are now a private pilot!

Starting immediately, you can now exercise all private pilot privileges. You can now rent an airplane, taking your friends or family for a flight anytime you want!

Next Steps

Getting a private pilot license is a very important step in your pilot career. It proves you can fly an airplane safely, thereby acting as the pilot in command of a small plane with passengers aboard. In other words, you can now be the captain in your own little plane.

Since you got your private pilot license, your skills have been validated by your flight instructor, possible check instructors, and the FAA examiner. Welcome to the small community of pilots!

Becoming a private pilot is an impressive accomplishment in itself, but it comes with some limitations. You aren't allowed to fly for compensation or hire. You can't work as a pilot or accept money, even if your friends want to pay you to take them somewhere.

That limitation is removed with the Commercial Pilot License (CPL), which is a completely separate pilot certificate that will replace your private pilot certificate once obtained.

Even more serious limitation for private pilots is that they are only allowed to fly in VMC. You can't fly through clouds, and you have to follow certain visibility requirements based on different airspaces.

This can be very limiting in areas that are often foggy or have low cloud layers. Because of this limitation, you may have to cancel many flights. There is an easy fix for this problem, however. You can get an Instrument Rating (IR) added to your private pilot license.

After receiving their private pilot licenses, most pilots start their instrument and commercial training at the same time. You can do alternating flights between the two curricula. Sometimes all your certificates and ratings can be included in one integrated curriculum, which depends on your training program.

Less time is required for the instrument training, so most pilots also complete the instrument rating check-ride before they get their commercial pilot license.

Next, let's talk about instrument training.

INSTRUMENT RATING - FAR 61.65 AND FAR 141 APPENDIX C

The private pilot certificate gives you the privilege to operate an aircraft only under VFR. You are not allowed to fly through clouds, so you need to keep a certain distance from them. You are also not allowed to fly if the visibility outside is below certain minimum criteria.

In order for you to remove these limitations, you will need an instrument rating added to your pilot license.

A rating is an authorization that sets forth special conditions, privileges, and/or limitations to your pilot certificate. An instrument rating authorizes you to operate an aircraft in Instrument Meteorological Conditions (IMC) and indicates that you can and are allowed to fly under IFR (instrument flight rules).

During your PPL training, you learned to fly mostly

by looking outside references to determine your aircraft attitude and location. You navigated by visual checkpoints on the ground and found your way around the traffic pattern by looking outside.

Instrument training will be different. You will do most of your training wearing a vision limiting device such as an instrument hood or glasses_specifically designed to block your peripheral view. These devices are designed to block your vision outside. You are forced to keep looking inside of the aircraft and fly with only instrument references. You don't have to worry about other air traffic because the air traffic controllers provide safe separation to instrument traffic. Moreover, your instructor will be your safety pilot looking outside when you are in VMC.

During instrument flight training, you will learn how to navigate using different types of electronic navigational aids used for navigating in low visibilities. Different airports use different types of instrument approaches. You will learn all about several types of approaches and how to fly them to find the runway. Standard Instrument Departures (SID) and Standard Instrument Arrival Procedures (STAR) are also covered in your training.

Instrument Rating is perhaps the most important pilot rating you can get. It will lift a lot of limitations that are otherwise applied to your pilot certificate. Even if you are not planning to fly commercially, I would recommend that you get this rating. Instrument flying skills can save your life if you inadvertently end up in IMC. An instrument rating will make you a better and safer pilot without question.

You can find the training requirements for an instrument rating from FAR 61.65,[1] and from FAR 141 Appendix C.[2] I will review those requirements next.

Instrument Rating Ground Training

If you train at a 141 school, your curriculum is going to include at least thirty hours of ground training in certain knowledge areas. Under 61 rules, you don't have any specific ground training requirements regarding specific hours.

Regardless of the school, you have to receive and log ground training or complete an authorized home-study course on certain aeronautical knowledge areas. Below is a list of the knowledge areas and a brief explanation about each of them:

1. **FARs that apply to flight operations under instrument flight rules (IFRs).** — The instrument rating

requirements can be found from FAR 61.65. You will also cover the Instrument Flight Rules from FAR 91.167 - 91.193[3] in detail.

2. **Appropriate information that applies to flight operations under IFR in the AIM.** — Instead of having a separate chapter for instrument procedures, the procedures are spread throughout the AIM. Each chapter has something that applies to instrument flying. Chapter one, for example, refers to different instrument navigation aids, while chapter nine references aeronautical charts, including IFR charts. The chapters between have other information relating to instrument flying. So, it's a good book to browse while focusing on the subjects which apply to your training. You can download the AIM for free,[4] as I have mentioned before.

3. **ATC systems and procedures for instrument flight operations.** — During your private pilot training, you had to do minimum communications with the ATC. If you trained in an uncontrolled airport you probably didn't talk to the ATC except during your cross-country flights.

During instrument training, however, you will be talking to the ATC during every flight. You will learn more about different ATC facilities and their functions. Moreover, you will learn about different procedures used for instrument flights and how they differ from VFR flights.

4. **IFR navigation and approaches by use of navigation systems.** — In ground school, you will talk about instrument navigation and approaches, so you understand how they work. You will further review these navigation methods, going into more details of instrument navigation systems such as VOR and GPS. Likewise, you will learn all about VOR, NDB, LOC, ILS, and GPS approaches, as well as some less common instrument approaches. Later on, this is where most of your flight training will focus. So, that's when you get to see how everything works in practice.

5. **Use of IFR en route and instrument approach procedure charts.** — At first glance, the instrument charts can be very confusing as they contain a lot of

numbers and abbreviations. Plus, they are mostly black and white. But you'll soon realize that, once you learn to read one approach chart, you can read them all in regard to the airport to which you are flying. En-route charts are fairly straight forward because they depict all the airways you can follow. Flight planning is actually easier with instrument charts compared to VFR charts since you don't need to think too hard what to choose as checkpoints. The checkpoints for instrument flying are something that you can identify with your navigation instruments — usually airway intersections, GPS fixes, or navigation facilities on the ground.

6. **Procurement and use of aviation weather reports and forecasts and the elements forecasting weather trends.** — You have already learned about weather theory and weather reports during your private pilot training. But it's such a broad subject that you'll dig deeper into it here. Now you'll be focusing on weather considerations relating to instrument flying obviously. For example, since you can now

fly inside the clouds, you need to be aware of rain and icing conditions which you may encounter.

7. **Safe and efficient operation of aircraft under instrument flight rules and conditions.** Safety first — again. An instrument rating will normally make you a safer pilot overall. However, unless you diligently follow established rules and procedures, you may put yourself at risk. This will be stressed throughout your training. Therefore, you better get used to it! Just like any other flight, a flight under IFR starts with proper preflight planning and checking that the weather is good enough for a safe flight. From there, you need to follow recommended safety practices during taxi, takeoff, cruise flight, approach, and landing. You will learn the specific procedures in your ground school first. Get ready to apply and practice them as you start flying.

8. **Recognition of critical weather situations and wind shear avoidance.** This is a topic that can't be stressed enough. You covered this during private pilot training, but since you can now

fly in clouds and rain, you might be attempted to take too many risks. You will review the topic here, and you will learn how to evaluate weather conditions more precisely. In instrument conditions, it's even more critical to recognize (and recover) from wind shear or other weather-related situations without delay. In IMC, you can't visually see any obstacles around you so swift action in critical situations is crucial.

9. **Aeronautical decision-making and judgment.** Being a good pilot all comes down to decision-making. You already talked about this in your private pilot training, but it will be reviewed here during instrument training. You will talk about decision making again during your commercial training and any other training you do later.

10. **Crew resource management, including crew communication and coordination.** Crew resource management (CRM) is a subject usually associated with multi-crew flying. All the same, it has played such an important role in reducing aviation accidents that the FAA wants to teach it early. CRM refers to the

use of all available resources to achieve a safe and efficient flight, and it was developed out of a need to address and mitigate human errors. You will learn the concepts of crew resource management; although, during the flight training, you will mostly focus on single-pilot resource management. Don't dismiss this topic, thinking it doesn't apply to you until you work in a multi-crew environment. The "crew" here applies, even if you are a single pilot crew. While CRM training normally focuses on working as a team in order to reduce accidents, it can be used for single-pilot operations as well. Even as a single pilot, you need to be able to manage the resources available to you. Only then can you improve your situational awareness and make better decisions. For example, when you are flying alone and running low on fuel and going to a busy airport, you should inform the ATC about your situation as soon as possible. ATC is a recource to you and they can give you priority over other traffic. CRM encompasses a wide range of skills and knowledge about pilot attitudes, communication, decision-making, situational awareness, and teamwork.

That's only ten knowledge areas, but the information is more focused and advanced than what you learned during your private pilot training. Some of the instrument flight rules and procedures can be a little difficult to comprehend at first. So, you need to put your head in the game and study hard!

All these knowledge areas are covered in FAA publications, which you can download for free. The first two topics are obviously covered in the FARs and the AIM. The other topics are covered in the following three manuals:

1. Instrument Flying Handbook[5]
2. Instrument Procedures Handbook[6]
3. Advanced Avionics Handbook[7]

All of them are free downloads, although you might want to get physical copies if you prefer paper. Those handbooks contain tons of information, including information that you won't be needing until you fly a more advanced aircraft. Before you start reading them from cover to cover, I would recommend you to download the Instrument Rating Airman Certification Standards (IR ACS),[8] and use it as a guide for your studies.

It's a booklet just like the PPL ACS. You can find all areas of knowledge, skills, and procedures which you need to demonstrate in your instrument rating check-ride. If you follow it systematically, you can easily keep track of your progress, thereby focusing on studying things with which you struggle.

The books you actually use in your ground school depends on the school at which you train. You might use Jeppesen Instrument / Commercial handbook,[9] for example, instead of the FAA handbooks. As long as you cover each subject and learn the required material, it doesn't matter which books you use.

Since the ground training is supposed to prepare you to take the instrument knowledge exam, you are likely to go through some sample questions in the class. Probably, you will also take occasional practice examinations.

If you train in a 141 school, you will probably have the same classmates you had during your PPL training. Those classmates will follow you through your commercial training and even flight instructor training if it's included in your program. If you train in a 61 school, you will normally do one-on-one training with your instructor, and you may not get to know other students that well.

Preparing for Instrument Rating Knowledge Exam

There are many good online study courses available for your instrument rating knowledge exam. Courses offered by Sporty's, Gleim, and AOPA can be excellent for helping to pass the knowledge exam. For instrument rating, you have one more study choice that was not available for PPL training. Sheppard Air[10] has probably the most up-to-date question banks and study software that can help you pass the exams. I used their software to study for my Airline Transport Pilot (ATP) exam, getting ninety-nine percent correct. Not bad at all!

These courses are not mandatory, of course. If you study in a 141 school, your ground school should be enough to train you for the exam. But it's good to check what other students or instructors recommend in your school. When I did my training in a 141 school, my training package included the Gleim question books for each of the certificates for which I was training. They didn't have online question banks at the time, so we used paperback study books instead. Your training package might include something similar, so it's better to check before you sign up for any additional courses.

Even if you follow one of the online study courses, make sure you actually study and understand all the material in the FAA handbooks. The online courses mostly focus on you passing the written exams, memorizing as many answers as you can – even if you don't understand the material. Memorizing the answers won't help you as a pilot, and it won't help you pass the checkride in the end.

Instrument Rating Knowledge Exam

Once you finish your ground training or self-study course, it's time to take the knowledge exam required for an instrument rating.

The knowledge exam is going to be a multiple-choice exam with sixty questions that you need to answer within 150 minutes (two and a half hours). That's exactly the same amount of questions and time as for the PPL examination.

The exam will randomly assign five questions from each of the following categories, except you will have ten questions from the weather category:

1. Regulations
2. IFR En Route and Approach Procedures
3. Air Traffic Control and Procedures
4. IFR Navigation
5. Weather Reports, Critical Weather, Windshear and Forecasts

6. Safe and Efficient IFR Operations
7. Aeronautical Decision-making
8. CRM

That's two fewer areas you will have to cover during your ground training. Essentially, these areas still cover the same information.

You can find detailed knowledge test requirements from the Instrument Rating Knowledge Test Guide.[11]

Flight Training for Instrument Rating

When you start your instrument flight training, you already know how to fly a plane at the private pilot level. Now you will learn to fly more precisely, following the indications of the flight instruments instead of flying by visual cues or outside references.

In a 141 school, you will need at least thirty-five hours of instrument flight training. In Part 61 schools, you need forty hours. Up to thirty hours (or fifty percent) of the training can be done in flight simulators or flight training devices. The actual time you are allowed to credit with simulators depends on your training curriculum, as well as the type of the simulator or flight training device available to you. In any case, training in a simulator can significantly reduce your training costs.

Your instrument flight training needs to cover the following areas of operation:

1. Pre-flight preparation;
2. Pre-flight procedures;
3. Air traffic control clearances and procedures;
4. Flight by reference to instruments;
5. Navigation systems;
6. Instrument approach procedures;
7. Emergency operations; and
8. Post-flight procedures.

There is at least one cross-country flight required for your instrument rating. The cross-country flight needs to be at least 250 nautical miles in total distance, including three different types of instrument approaches. One of the flight segments during this flight needs to be at least a hundred nautical miles straight line distance.

Another requirement under 61 rules is that, as a pilot in command, you need to log fifty hours of cross-country flight time for the rating. That might sound a lot, but if you complete your commercial flight training along with instrument training, then you can log those hours quickly. Also, any cross-country flights you do as a private pilot would count towards the requirement.

However, it means that you can't just get your private pilot license, and then get then instrument rating by doing forty hours of instrument training. In essence, you can't get your instrument rating right away. You will have to do some cross-country flying as a private pilot before you can do the instrument rating checkride.

The cross-country flights don't have to be solo cross-country flights. As a private pilot, you can have passengers with you. Also, this fifty hours of cross-country flying rule applies to you only if you train in a Part 61 school.

I did my training in a 141 school, so there was no such requirement. I suppose the reasoning behind this was that the FAA knows the students in 141 schools are going to do their commercial pilot training anyway. Therefore, they get lots of experience and training that way.

In 61 schools, the student may only get the instrument rating added to his or her private pilot license and then just fly for fun. They don't want private pilots without any actual cross-country experience flying in more demanding instrument conditions.

Instrument Flight Training Progress

Just like private pilot training, your instrument flight training will also be structured to follow a certain curriculum. My instrument training involved three different stages and three different stage checks. Your curriculum may not require any stage checks, but you will still have to learn all the same skills and procedures.

For the training to be effective, you will start with simple tasks. Once you master the basics, you move on to more advanced procedures. Even if your curriculum is not split into separate stages, you should be following a step-by-step process that builds on previously learned skills.

Next, I will describe the three stages of a typical instrument rating curriculum.

Stage 1 - Basic Instrument Flying

The first part of instrument training is usually spent in your local training area. You are not going to jump directly to flying instrument approaches. Instead, you are going back to basics. You will learn to do basic flying and flight maneuvers while wearing a view limiting device. Flying by instrument references is called attitude instrument flying. I did my training wearing an instrument hood, but there are other options available as well. I have introduced some of the most common view limiting devices in my flight training page.[12]

It's easy to get mentally disoriented in instrument flight conditions. Your body sensations may tell you that you are turning one way while you are actually flying straight and level or turning the other way. That's why, while in the first stage of training, you will focus on basic flying with instrument references only. This will improve your instrument scanning technique, and you will learn to trust the instruments.

Primary and Secondary Instruments

When you focus on observing the flight instruments, it will clarify the meaning and purpose of each instrument and its indications. You will learn what your primary and secondary instruments are for level flight, turning, climbing, descending, etc.

During your PPL training, you already learned about the six main airplane instruments. The six instruments are airspeed indicator, artificial horizon (or attitude indicator), altimeter, turn coordinator, heading indicator, and vertical speed indicator. They can be separate old analog instruments (often referred as the six-pack), or they can all be presented in one modern glass-cockpit screen.

As a private pilot, you already know how the instruments work. Still, you may not have been scanning them properly to get the information needed for precise flying. For example, what does the airspeed indicator tell you other than your speed? Well, if the speed is increasing and you are not touching the throttle, it means your aircraft is pitching down. Alternatively, it means you are pitching up if the airspeed is decreasing. This can then be verified from the altimeter, vertical speed indicator, and the artificial horizon.

As a second example: If the heading indicator is moving, it would tell you that the aircraft is banking to one direction or the other. Then. you would look at your turn coordinator and the artificial horizon to verify the information.

All the instruments have several uses. Therefore, you need to be scanning all of them during each phase of flight. You will learn how to properly scan and cross-check each instrument at proper times. You will further learn about instrument errors and limitations.

Partial Panel Flying and Compass Turns

At times, your instructor will cover up some of the

instruments such as the heading indicator or artificial horizon to simulate instrument failures. That's called partial panel flying, and it will improve your instrument flying skills.

When the heading indicator is covered, you will learn how to do compass turns to different headings. Using a free-floating compass for turns is a bit more complicated than it sounds. Unlike a heading indicator moving at the same rate as the airplane turns, the compass either leads or lags the turn. Depending on the heading, you may have to roll out up to thirty degrees before or after the heading for which you are looking. You will learn all this fun stuff and more on the ground before you get in the air. Mastering compass turns is one of the important skills you will learn in stage one.

Timed Turns

You will also learn how to do turns to different heading by timing the turn. These turns are called 'timed turns.' Under instrument conditions, you are normally expected to do 'standard rate turns' by following your instruments. In a standard rate, you will turn three degrees per second, meaning it takes 120 seconds or two minutes to make a 360-degree turn. Learning to use a timer while you fly is important preparation for flying approaches and holding procedures later in training.

During timed turns your instructor may briefly cover both, the heading indicator and the compass. During the turns you would focus your attention to the turn coordinator and your timer in order to turn to desired headings. For a 180-degree you would time it for one minute, for 90-degree turn thirty seconds, and so on. For small 10-degree turns you could simply count to three instead of using the timer.

Unusual Attitudes

As I mentioned, it's easy to get disoriented when you are in instrument conditions. That's why it's also easy to enter unusual attitudes unintentionally. An unusual attitude is any attitude exceeding normal pitch or bank angles. It's usually something you enter unintentionally. For example, you may get close to stall while turning and pitching up. Conversely, you may move into a nose dive if you don't hold enough back-pressure during a turn. If you enter an unusual attitude, you need to know how to recognize it and how to recover from this attitude, and transition back to normal flight. You will practice these recoveries with your instructor.

During unusual attitude training, your instructor

will ask you to close your eyes for a moment. When you open your eyes again, the aircraft might be nose high, close to a stall, or it might be diving down towards the ground. You will learn the proper techniques on how to bring the airplane back to level flight to avoid any accidents. While it's important for you to learn how to recover from these attitudes, it's even more important for you to learn how to avoid them from happening. You need to learn how to constantly observe your instruments to avoid unusual attitudes.

Other Maneuvers

Stall recoveries, slow flight, and steep turns are also practiced in this stage. Everything is done while wearing a view limiting device. You wouldn't do steep turns in actual instrument conditions, but it's necessary to practice them in case you need to do them in abnormal situations in IMC. Stall recoveries give you practice for safety purposes and slow flight, on the other hand, it is a basic maneuver that you may have to do during normal instrument approaches.

Instrument Patterns

If you have a flight training device or a simulator

available, you may use them to fly certain instrument patterns, as seen in this document by Gleim.[13] https://www.gleim.com/public/pdf/av_updates/ipfmadd2.pdf

You can do them in a real airplane also, but I think the time is better used in a simulator. I remember flying the Patterns A and B early in my training. I also used the patterns while teaching my instrument students.

Those instrument flying patterns combine instrument flying skills such as: flying timed turns, procedure turns, and changing aircraft configurations. If you do these in a simulator, you can print out your pattern at the end of the flight. The goal is to make it look like the original, which won't be easy, especially if you fly it partial panel!

Flying those patterns may feel meaningless, but they are a good way to improve your instrument scan and using the timer. It enhances your overall ability to fly the plane smoothly in instrument conditions before you start flying actual instrument approaches.

Basic Instrument Procedures

Once you get the handle of the basic instrument flight skills, you will move onto some basic instrument procedures. You might have already done this while flying in and out of the airport area, but you will learn to intercept and track different radials or bearings from ground facilities or satellite fixes. Depending on your curriculum, you might also learn to fly DME Arcs (DME stands for Distance Measuring Equipment) that are sometimes part of instrument approaches. DME Arc is a constant distance arc around a ground facility.

The first stage of the training shouldn't take long. If you train in a 61 school, you may just do a couple of flight practicing compass turns, timed turns, unusual attitudes, and some basic maneuvers. Then, you move onto flying instrument approaches. In a 141 school, you probably have an easy stage check after a few flight lessons. Just like during PPL training, the stage checks are just reviews of what you have learned so far.

Stage Two — SIDs, STARs, Approaches and Holding Procedures

When you start your second stage of instrument training, you should already be able to control the aircraft accurately by instrument references. Essentially, you should be able to make smooth standard rate turns, maintain a constant airspeed, and maintain altitude within a hundred feet or so. The better you are at controlling the airplane, the easier it is to focus on the new procedures that are introduced in this stage.

In this stage, you will learn to fly different:

- Standard Instrument Departures (SID)
- Standard Terminal Arrival Routes (STAR)
- Instrument Approach Procedures
- Holding Procedures

Next, I will describe each topic one by one.

Standard Instrument Departures

SIDs are air routes that will safely take you away from the airport. They are designed to simplify the flight clearance procedures and to keep aircraft away from terrain.

Flying the departures involves tracking and intercepting radials or bearings from ground facilities. If you fly a GPS equipped training aircraft, you can also fly departure procedures based on GPS waypoints.

In addition to providing a route to fly, the SIDs also provide you with a vertical path to follow. The vertical path can require you to meet certain climb gradient if there are obstacles around, or sometimes the SIDs may require a steeper climb gradient for noise abatement purposes. Climb gradient is not required by all SIDs, however, and small training aircraft don't usually have to worry too much about noise abatement. What is required by all instrument departures is to follow certain altitudes at specific waypoints.

Standard Terminal Arrival Routes

STARs are similar procedures as SIDs, except that they are routes that guide you back to the airport instead of away from there. When talking about STARs, most people simply call them arrivals.

The instrument arrivals normally join with the different approaches that are available at the airport. This again simplifies the clearance procedures and pilot workload when operating near the airport as all IFR traffic can follow the same routes.

You will learn how to fly different SIDs and STARs during your training, at least in theory. Although, you may not actually fly them every time you leave or enter air airport airspace. Most of the time, you are likely to follow vectors (directions given by the air traffic controllers) or specific headings issued by the ATC instead of flying the arrival or departure procedures.

That's because those procedures typically connect with airways, taking you to higher altitudes that are not meant for piston-powered light aircraft. The first time I started actually flying SIDs and STARs was when I got a job in corporate aviation. Before that, there was never a real reason to follow one of those procedures. In any case, you will get the idea how the procedures work and how to read the charts.

Instrument Approach Procedures

Your training's main focus in the second stage will be flying different types of instrument approaches. Operating under instrument conditions makes it relatively easy to find the airport by using your navigation instruments. The critical part of the flight, however, is joining an approach, flying it, and landing from an instrument approach.

The approach will take you all the way to the landing end of an active runway or to a certain point, called a missed approach point, before the runway. Once you reach the specified minimum altitude, you will have to land the aircraft visually or execute a missed approach.

In general, instrument approaches are divided into precision approaches, approaches with vertical guidance, and non-precision approaches.

Precision approaches, such as ILS approaches, provide you with a lateral course to fly as well as glide slope or a vertical descent angle to take you to the runway. ILS approaches are the most common precision approaches out there. Probably ninety-nine percent of all approaches that I do are ILS approaches; although, that's probably because I do most of my flying in Asia. I know people flying in the US, and they do a lot of visual or GPS approaches instead of ILS approaches.

ILS approaches are most likely the only precision approaches that you will practice during your training. Although, you will learn about other types of approaches such as the Precision Approach Radar (PAR) approaches.

It's a fantastic feeling to make an instrument approach through a thick layer of clouds or fog, and emerging from the weather just 200 feet above the ground with the runway in front of you! It's unlikely, though, that you will do much of your training in actual instrument conditions. Instead, you will fly the approaches wearing a view limiting device. Once you reach the minimum altitude, your instructor will tell you to look outside and land the plane. At this point, you will only have a few seconds to get oriented with the outside references which can make it an exciting landing!

Approaches with vertical guidance are similar to precision approaches. Except, they take you to different minimum altitudes and may have different visibility requirements.

These types of approaches include Localizer Type Direction Aid (LDA) approaches and the increasingly common Area Navigation (RNAV) or GPS approaches.

Non-precision approaches provide you with course guidance, but won't give you vertical guidance to bring the aircraft down. It's up to the pilot to plan the descent so that the plane arrives at a proper altitude for landing at a specific distance from the airport. Minimum Descent Altitudes (MDA) and visibility requirements are higher in non-precision approaches than in precision approaches.

The most common non-precision approaches that you will practice are NDB approaches, and VOR approaches.

These types of approaches are becoming less and less common. While flying a corporate jet aircraft around the world for over seven years, I have done only a handful of actual VOR approaches during the whole time. And, as far as I can remember, I have done only one actual NDB approach outside my training. You will still have to learn and practice them, though. VORs and NDBs are still in use in many airports around the world – at least as backups.

Holding Procedures

Sometimes airports experience delays due to bad weather or for other reasons. When this happens, air traffic control has to ask approaching airplanes to slow down, thereby accommodating the traffic flow. Sometimes they even have to ask airplanes to hold over specified fixes or points.

Unlike a car, you can't just stop and pull over on the side of a road. Instead, there are standardized holding procedures that pilots have to follow when requested. A standard holding pattern is basically an asymmetrical race track pattern that has a starting and ending point over a ground facility or a GPS waypoint.

You will learn how to fly the patterns symmetrically so that you stay within a specified area. This is done either by timing your inbound and outbound legs or by using DME. Moreover, it involves applying proper wind correction based on the wind at your holding altitude.

There are three ways you can enter a holding pattern: 1. Direct entry; 2. Parallel entry; and 3. Teardrop entry.[14] The entry method for each holding pattern depends on the direction you are coming from. Determining the proper entry method can be confusing initially, but there are some easy methods to figure it out. You will learn all about them during your training.

Overall, this is a fun stage. All these procedures may sound complicated when you study the theory behind them. But when you fly them, it can be easier than you expected.

All the procedures are designed to keep the airplanes safe, reducing pilot and controller workload. It's your responsibility to follow the procedures and trust your aircraft instruments. It's essential to fly the proce-dures exactly as they are depicted on your paper or elec-tronic charts. All this is much easier if your basic aircraft handling skills are up to standard. Moreover, it's easier if your instructor briefs you properly before and after each flight.

When you fly the approaches, you will also have to do many radio calls to the ATC. You will have to write down clearances and read them back. In the beginning, your instructor is likely to help you. But in the end, you will have to do all that by yourself while still flying the plane. After all, you are training for single-pilot operations.

You are likely to fly all possible types of instrument approaches that are available in your local and nearby airports. The more different approaches you practice, the better.

After you are proficient at flying all the approaches and other instrument procedures required by this stage, you will have another stage check (if required by your curriculum).

During this stage check you are likely to do at least one precision approach and two other types of approaches. You also have to demonstrate some holding pattern entries and a few holding turns. Again, the purpose is just to review your progress at this stage.

Stage Three - Instrument Cross Country Flights

Towards the end of your instrument training, you will need to do at least one cross-country flight. It's a dual cross-country as there are no solo flights in instrument training. If you train in a 61 school, you might already have done this flight, but in 141 schools, you usually do it at the end of the training.

Before you commence the cross-country flight, you should already have practiced different approach procedures. On this flight, you need to do three different types of instrument approaches, and you should be familiar with the procedures before you go to new airports.

The cross-country flight needs to be at least 250 nautical miles in total distance. One of the flight segments needs to be at least a hundred nautical miles, straight-line distance.

Instrument cross-country flights are actually easier than visual ones. You won't have to be looking out and try to find your checkpoints. Instead, you find your checkpoints by looking at your instruments. They can be intersections of airways that you find by intercepting radials from different ground stations or by measuring the distance from ground stations. If you have a GPS-equipped aircraft, then you can also use satellite fixes as your waypoints.

During the cross-country your instructor will still be looking outside for other air traffic, especially if you are flying in VMC. But you'll be wearing an instrument hood or another type of view limiting device for most of the flight.

My instrument cross-country flight took us four and a half hours to complete. We did a total of four approaches during the flight, with one being a missed approach. We also did some holding practice before returning home.

I remember it being quite tiring because I was wearing an instrument hood most of the time, and I had to focus on staring at the instruments all the time. There was another student in the backseat, so at least we had some conversation going to pass the time.

Back-Seating Other Flights

'Back-seating' other flights can be beneficial for you as well. When you sit in the backseat as another student is training, you can get a better overall picture of what is happening. You can see what the instructor sees around the aircraft, and you can follow the procedures by looking at the instruments and paper charts. This will improve your situational awareness, and it's a great way to get some free extra instruction. It will also provide you with a different perspective of flying when you observe how other students perform.

If you do some back-seating, it's a good idea also to ask to attend the pre- and post-flight briefings. This will help you get a complete picture of what to expect from the flight, as well as what to look for when the other student is flying. You will additionally learn a lot from the instructor's critique at the end of the flight.

All this, of course, has to be approved by both the instructor and the student. It might be better to check with your fellow students first on whether they mind you back-seating. Not every student likes to be observed like that, and they are the ones paying for the training after all.

Fifty Hours Cross-Country Time

Once you complete the required instrument cross-country flight, you should meet all the requirements for the practical exam. However, if you train in a 61 school, you would need fifty hours of cross-country time before you can take the exam. The fifty hours can be VFR flights and don't have to be part of your instrument training.

It's common to do commercial flight training at the same time with instrument training. So, getting the hours shouldn't be a problem. You should time your training so that you have the fifty cross-country hours by the time you are planning to take your instrument checkride.

Final Stage Check

The last flight in the instrument flight curriculum is

usually the final stage check. In the final stage check, you will review everything you have learned during the course. You will need to prepare for it properly, as it is like a simulated checkride.

As long as you meet the standards and are comfortable with everything in the IR ACS, you are ready. If you feel like you struggle with something, then you might need extra training. But if you have made it this far following a proper training syllabus, then there should be no reason for extra flight training.

In the final stage check, you will cover all the training area maneuvers such as unusual attitudes, stall recoveries, slow flight, compass turns, timed turns, etc. After that, you will do a few different approaches, holding procedures, missed approaches, and finally a full-stop landing. If you pass, the next step is the checkride!

Instrument Pilot Practical Exam

The instrument checkride is usually just like the final stage check. It will have two parts — the oral exam and the flight exam.

If you have systematically studied each knowledge area regarding the airmen certification standards, then the oral exam should be fairly easy.

At this point, you are already a certificated pilot. So, your accumulated aviation knowledge and understanding of flight instruments and procedures should have increased significantly since your PPL checkride.

In any case, the instrument oral exam guide[15] can help you brush up on some instrument knowledge during the days before your checkride. I know some instructors and examiners frown upon those guides. They only give you short answers and minimum knowledge, but nevertheless, they contain tons of factual information.

The flight part of your checkride will be just about the same as your final stage check. You might start it by pretending to go for an instrument cross-country flight that the examiner cuts short after a couple of checkpoints. Then, you will do some maneuvers in a training area, finishing off the checkride with different types of instrument approaches. This is followed by a full-stop landing. My instrument checkride took me 1.3 hours (one hour and eighteen minutes). So, it wasn't too long.

After the flight, you will have a post-flight briefing. The examiner will print you your temporary private pilot certificate with an instrument rating added to it. Congratulations! You can now fly in the clouds!

Maintaining the Currency of Your Instrument Rating

The instrument rating is a very important rating. You can't fly professionally without it — unless, of course, you only do VFR flying such a banner towing. The instrument procedures can sometimes be confusing. If you don't fly in IMC much, it's easy to forget the proper instrument flight skills. That's why the instrument rating comes with some strict currency requirements.

Once you get the rating, you need to maintain your 'instrument currency.' To stay current, you will need to fly at least six instrument approaches every six months. You need to further complete holding procedures and intercept and track radials. Otherwise, you can't fly as a pilot in command in IMC.

If you don't maintain your currency, you won't lose your rating completely; you just can't use it. To make it valid again, you will have to do an Instrument Proficiency Check (IPC) with a certified instructor. The IPC can usually be done in a simulator or a real aircraft, depending on the equipment available to you. The IPC is a review of all necessary instrument procedures and approaches required to operate aircraft safely in IMC.

It's still better to get the rating as soon as possible once you get your private pilot license. Just be mindful that you need to keep it current, or you might have to do some instrument proficiency checks later.

You can find the exact currency requirements from eCFR 61.57 - Recent Flight Experience: Pilot in Command.[16]

COMMERCIAL PILOT CERTIFICATE - FAR 61 SUBPART F AND FAR 141 APPENDIX D

You need to get a commercial pilot certificate if you want to earn money flying as a professional pilot. This certificate is required from any pilot planning to fly for compensation or hire — no matter whether it's flight instructing, banner towing, crop dusting, cargo-, or passenger flying you are planning to do. You'll still need to get your commercial pilot certificate. The certificate is also often called commercial pilot license (CPL).

Just like instrument training, you can start your CPL training immediately after you have passed your PPL checkride. Often times, pilots do the CPL and IR training at the same time to mix things up.

During instrument training, you focused on observing the flight instruments, and it's easy to forget the importance of looking outside for other air traffic. Commercial flight training, however, is mostly visual training. And so, you'll be looking at outside references most of the time.

When you do commercial and instrument training together, it can be very beneficial. The flight skills you learn during commercial training will help you better control the aircraft during instrument training, and the instrument flight skills will help you during your commercial flights as well, especially during your commercial cross countries.

You need to be at least eighteen years old when you take your CPL checkride. So, if you got your private pilot certificate and instrument rating at the seventeen years old, you might have to wait a few months before you can get the commercial pilot license.

Commercial flight training is all about gaining more experience and getting more precise with your flight skills. A few new flight maneuvers are introduced to improve your skills, while old maneuvers are practiced to stricter standards. You will also be introduced to a "complex" or a "technically advanced" aircraft that is a slightly bigger and advanced aircraft than what you used for your private pilot training.

In commercial ground school, you dig deeper into

many same areas of operations you have previously studied. I will discuss the commercial ground school next.

Commercial Pilot Ground Training

In 141 schools, you are required to receive at least 35 hours of ground training. In 61 schools... you guessed it; there is no specific hour requirement for ground training.

But again, regardless of the school, you would have to receive and log ground training, or complete an authorized home study course on the following aeronautical knowledge areas:

1. **Applicable FARs that relate to commercial pilot privileges, limitations, and flight operations.** Same as with any other certificate or rating. First, you need to know the rules and regulations that apply to the certification with which you are seeking. You can find the commercial regulations pilot from FAR Part 61, Subpart F - Commercial Pilots. [1]

2. **Accident reporting requirements of the NTSB.** As a private pilot, it's important to understand accident reporting

requirements to the NTSB. It's more critical for commercial pilots who may operate multi-million dollar equipment, and may be in charge of multiple passenger lives. During commercial training, you will also cover this topic in more detail than during private pilot training.

3. **Basic aerodynamics and the principles of flight.** At this point, basic aerodynamics and principles of flight are probably still fresh in your mind. During commercial flight training, however, you are likely to talk more about how aerodynamics apply to bigger, more complex, airplanes.

4. **Meteorology to include recognition of critical weather situations, wind shear recognition and avoidance, and the use of aeronautical weather reports and forecasts.** I can't stress enough how important the subject of weather is. There are countless examples of aircraft accidents caused by weather (and bad decision making). This is why you will review the topic here and frequently throughout your career. You will also learn to review weather reports before each flight,

so you can recognize any critical weather situations in advance.

5. **Safe and efficient operation of aircraft.** You will be responsible for the safety of your passengers as a commercial pilot, which is a huge responsibility. Safe operations are emphasized at all times during your training. Efficiency is also essential for all commercial operators. It's all about fuel savings in the commercial air transportation business. You will learn about the optimum cruise altitudes and power settings for your aircraft, etc.

6. **Weight and balance computations**. Weight and balance computations for bigger aircraft are usually more complicated. You will really have to consider how to load your cargo or where to seat your passengers. Moreover, you will have to consider how fuel burn will affect your weight and balance before landing.

7. **Use of performance charts.** Most pilots dread this topic. There are countless charts, tables, and diagrams you need to learn how to use and read. Most of them are very straight forward, but some charts can be

complicated and confusing. With more complex airplanes, most of the performance calculations are done by the flight management computers. Therefore, the pilot workload is significantly reduced. As a pilot, you still need to know how to do all the calculations manually. All airplane manufacturers publish performance charts and tables that can be used to make the calculations. You will learn how to calculate takeoff and landing distances, takeoff and climb performance, stall speeds, cruise distances, brake cooling times, etc. These are all based on different aircraft configurations and weather. It's all very easy with the training airplanes you use, but once you start flying bigger passenger aircrafts, the charts usually get more complicated.

8. **Significance and effects of exceeding aircraft performance and limitations.** Obviously you should never exceed aircraft performance and limitations. You will discuss possible wear and tear that can happen to your aircraft if you exceed the limitations. You may further review some accidents caused by pilots who

exceeded certain limitations or didn't meet a specific flight's performance requirements.

9. **Use of aeronautical charts and a magnetic compass for pilotage and dead reckoning**. At this point, using aeronautical charts will be old news to you. The key point here is using the magnetic compass. Unlike the heading indicator generally used for maintaining headings, the magnetic compass floats freely and is subject to errors. If you started your instrument training before commercial training, then you already know about compass turns and compass errors. And you already know about pilotage and dead reckoning from your private pilot cross-country flights. Here you go into more detail about discussing the earth's magnetic fields and how your latitude affects the compass. You will also review concepts such as magnetic variation, true headings, and magnetic headings.

10. **Use of air navigation facilities**. This is more of a review of previously learned material. But you'll get to review your knowledge about all the navigational facilities available to you.

11. **Aeronautical decision making and judgment**. As I mentioned before, you will review decision making and judgment here. Being a good pilot is all about making good decisions based on all available information. Decision-making is an important topic that you can apply to everything else you do in life. Basically, you will learn to think more critically about every decision you have to make.

12. **Principles and functions of aircraft systems**. You may end up flying multiple types of aircraft as a commercial pilot. While you may only fly piston airplanes during your training, you will also learn the basics of turbo-prop and jet aircraft systems. You share the airspace with countless types of aircraft, so it's good to understand the basics of how they operate. The primary focus will still be on the systems of your training airplane, especially if you're doing your commercial training in a different type of aircraft than what you used to fly.

13. **Maneuvers, procedures, and emergency operations appropriate to the aircraft**. During commercial flight

training, you will learn new maneuvers such as lazy-eights, eights on pylons, chandelles, and steep spirals. Emergency procedures and other procedures for your training aircraft may differ from what you are used to by this point. You will learn all the theory behind all this before you have to apply the procedures in the air.

14. **Night and high-altitude operations**. You will have to do solo night flights during commercial flight training. Reviewing the theory behind night flights is essential before flying at night. You need to be comfortable with your expectations before you attempt a solo night flight. You won't be doing any high altitude flying in a piston plane, but since you are studying to become a commercial pilot, you will have to learn the theory behind high altitude flying. This includes studying high altitude meteorology, physiological effects of high altitude flight and oxygen requirements, high altitude aerodynamics and aircraft systems, etc.

15. **Procedures for operating within the National Airspace System**. You are more likely to fly to the nation's busiest

airports and airspaces while working as a commercial pilot. Moreover, you may operate in high altitudes and/or fly international flights. This topic discusses procedures and requirements for entering and operating in different airspaces.

Many of the subject areas are similar to subject areas which you covered in your private pilot training. The PPL ground school, however, only scratched the surface of most of the topics. In CPL ground training, you will dig deeper into each knowledge area while covering the material more thoroughly.

Commercial Pilot Knowledge Exam

To study for the knowledge exam, I would recommend you use the same study materials you used for your PPL and/or IR studies, if you were happy with them. The study course by Sheppard Air is probably the easiest way to study and pass the exam. That is, of course, in addition to your commercial ground school training.

The FAA commercial pilot knowledge exam has a hundred multiple-choice questions, and the required score to pass is seventy percent. Easy!

The exam has a nearly equal amount of questions from each of the following knowledge areas:

1. Regulations
2. Accident Reporting
3. Aerodynamics
4. Meteorology - Weather
5. Safe and Efficient Operations
6. Weight and Balance
7. Performance Charts
8. Aircraft Limitations
9. Pilotage and Dead Reckoning
10. AIR Navigation Facilities
11. Aeronautical Decision-Making (ADM)
12. Aircraft Systems
13. Maneuvers, Procedures, Emergency Operations
14. Night and High Altitude Operations
15. NAS Operations (National Airspace Systems)

You only need to be sixteen years old to take the written exam. So, you can get it out of the way long before you are even allowed to take the CPL practical exam. You can find more information about the CPL

Exam from the Commercial Pilot Knowledge Test Guide.[2]

Commercial Flight Training

Commercial flight training is relatively low-stress training compared to private pilot and instrument training. You already have your private pilot license, so you know how to fly a plane. During commercial flight training, you focus on improving your previously learned skills to higher standards and gain more flight experience.

You usually get a single-engine commercial pilot license first, and later add a multi-engine rating onto it. Single engine-commercial pilots need to receive training and become proficient in the following areas of operations:

1. Pre-flight preparation
2. Pre-flight procedures
3. Airport operations
4. Takeoffs, landings, and go-arounds
5. Performance maneuvers
6. Ground reference maneuvers
7. Navigation
8. Slow flight and stalls

9. Emergency operations
10. High-altitude operations, and
11. Postflight procedures

You can find details regarding the proficiency requirements from the Commercial Pilot Airman Certification Standards (CPL ACS)[3]. If you do your initial commercial checkride in a multi-engine aircraft, there will be additional requirements. I will discuss multi-engine training as an add-on rating later in this book.

Aeronautical Experience Requirements

In addition to becoming proficient with flight skills, you will have some specific aeronautical experience requirements.

In 141 schools, the course will consist of 120 hours of flight training. Thirty percent of the hours can be in simulators.

In 61 schools, you will have to log 250 hours before you can take the checkride. This time can include all your previous training and flying. Also, only a hundred of those 250 hours have to be in powered aircraft, meaning you can log some time in non-powered aircraft such as gliders. The 250 hours also need to include at least a hundred hours pilot-in-command time and fifty hours cross country time.

You can find all the detailed requirements from FAR 61.129[4] and FAR 141 Appendix D.[5] In 141 schools, it's easy to keep track of the times by following the curriculum. If you train in a 61 school, you should personally pay attention to make sure you meet all the time requirements as you may not follow an FAA approved curriculum.

Dual Training

In 141 schools, you will need at least fifty-five hours of flight training with an instructor. For part 61 students, the hour requirement is only twenty hours. Regardless of the school, those hours have to include at least the following:

- Ten hours of instrument flight training;
- Ten hours of flight training in a complex airplane, a turbine-powered airplane, or a technically advanced airplane;
- One two-hour DAY cross-country flight with straight line distance of at least a hundred nautical miles;
- One two-hour NIGHT cross-country flight

with straight line distance of at least a
hundred nautical miles;
- Three hours in a single-engine airplane in
  preparation for the practical test within sixty
  days preceding the date of test.

The training also needs to cover all the flight proficiency areas of operations that were mentioned earlier.

Solo Training

You will need to log at least ten hours of solo flight time during your commercial training. Alternatively, it can be pilot-in-command time with an authorized instructor on board. But most commercial training curricula make it solo training, which saves money for the students. Even when you are the pilot-in-command, you would have to pay for the instructor's fee if there is an instructor on board.

The ten hours need to include the following:

- One long cross-country flight with one
  segment of at least 250 nautical miles in
  straight line distance.
- Five hours night flight in VFR conditions

with ten takeoffs and ten landings at an
airport with an operating control tower.

Most commercial students end up doing much more
than ten hours of solo flying during commercial training.
Ten hours is only the minimum solo flight requirement,
but it makes more financial sense to maximize the solo
flights and minimize the dual flight hours. So, you save
on the instructor fees.

For example, if you train in a 141 school, you need
120 total flight training hours. Fifty-five of the 120 hours
need to be dual training, meaning you can do up to sixty-
five hours of solo flight training. Although only ten hours
is required.

Commercial Training Progress

The commercial training curriculum is usually
divided into three or more stages, each followed by stage
checks. Of course, in part 61 schools, this may not be the
case. In part 61 schools, you may do the training in whatever order you like. I'm sure you got the idea of how the
61 and 141 schools differ by now.

In 141 schools, I have seen the training divided
usually into three or four stages. Here is a brief description of a typical three-stage structure:

Stage One - Commercial Maneuvers and Dual Night Flights

In addition to practicing already learned maneuvers up to commercial standards, you will need to learn a few new flight maneuvers. The new maneuvers include:

- **Chandelles** – Maximum performance, 180-degree, climbing turn which helps you develop your coordination and aircraft handling skills.
- **Lazy Eights** – Series of climbing and descending turns in a coordinated fashion. A maneuver designed to improve your coordination, orientation, planning, and division of attention.
- **Eights on Pylons** – Basically a figure eight around two points on the ground. Designed to help you control the aircraft in low altitudes while dividing your attention between outside cues and flight instruments.
- **Steep Spirals** – A combination of spiraling descent and turns around a ground reference point.
- **Power-Off 180 Accuracy Approaches and Landings** – Improves

your skills for planning and accurately executing a safe power-off emergency landing.

Most of these maneuvers are explained in the Airplane Flying Handbook chapter 9 in detail, and with images (I hope you have downloaded it by now from funkypilot.com/resources).

The main purpose of practicing all those maneuvers is to improve your overall flight, coordinations, and division of attention skills. Practicing chandelles also has a practical purpose, especially if you fly in a mountainous area where you might have to make climbing turns away from the mountains. Power-off 180 accuracy approaches help you in case of an emergency landing. Lazy eights and eights on pylons may not have a practical purpose other than improving your flight skills. At least, I can't think of any pilot job (other than instructing) where you would be flying around making figure eights in the air!

You will keep practicing previously learned maneuvers such as steep turns, slow flight, and stall recoveries up to commercial pilot standards. All these are stricter than private pilot standards. By different standards, I mean, you need to maintain airspeeds, bank angles, and altitudes within tighter limits during the maneuvers.

Stage one of the commercial training will focus on

learning the new maneuvers with your instructor first. After that, you will practice them on your own during solo flights. You may also do some dual night flights in this stage. Later on, you will need to do solo night flights, but it's better to improve your nighttime flight skills with an instructor aboard first.

Approaches and landings at night can subject you to many different visual illusions. These can be dangerous unless you have a solid understanding of them. No worries, though; your instructor will make sure you will be thoroughly prepared for your solo night flights.

Once you have reached all the objectives of this stage, you will have a stage check giving you an opportunity to fly with a check instructor again. Just like with other stage checks, you will have to review everything you learned during this particular stage.

Stage Two - Solo Night Flights and Hour Building

During the second stage of your commercial flight training, you do quite a lot of solo flying. At this point, you are already an experienced pilot. Flight preparation is easy, and day time solo flights will feel like routine missions. Solo flights are still going to be exciting, but I bet most of the nervousness you felt during your first solos will be gone. Pre-flight preparation and flying out to practice areas will feel like second nature. So, fly out there and practice whatever maneuvers are required by your curriculum.

Based on aircraft availability in your flight school, you can now do more frequent flights because you won't have to adjust your schedule to instructor availability. Just keep flying two or three flights every day if you can, and you'll be done with the commercial training before you know it!

Two or three flights daily may sound like a lot of work compared to doing one longer flight once a day. But I can assure you that the more full flight cycles you do, the more competent and comfortable you will get with flying.

Since you are the one paying for the flight hours, I would recommend you to split it between several flights to get the most rewarding experience. Although, you might want to save some flight hours for possible extra solo cross-country flights if there are some airports nearby that you would like to visit – and if your flight school allows you to fly to them.

Furthermore, this flight stage includes practicing maneuvers in local training areas, practicing different types of takeoffs and landings in the traffic pattern, and completing any required cross-country flights.

This is also the time to complete your night solo

flights, at least five hours of it. If your flight school is based on an uncontrolled airfield, you will have to do at least one night flight to an airport with an operating control tower, and complete ten takeoffs and landings there.

When I did my commercial training, I had to do a solo night flight from the uncontrolled Conway Airport in South Carolina to a controlled Myrtle Beach airport. In Myrtle Beach, I completed the required ten takeoffs and landings. Obviously, I also had to fly back to Conway the same night. So, I ended up doing eleven takeoffs and landings during that night. It was fun flying, and the toughest thing was probably keeping track of the number of landings!

Stage Three — Complex Training or Technically Advanced Aircraft Training

Things will get more interesting once you reach the last stage of your commercial training. You will do ten hours of training in a "complex" airplane, which is an airplane with retractable landing gear, flaps, and a controllable pitch propeller. Well, this at least used to be the case until the FAA changed some requirements in 2018.

For a long time, there was a requirement for ten hours of complex training for commercial pilots. There was also a requirement to do part of the practical examination in a complex airplane to demonstrate the ability to retract and extend the landing at appropriate times.

However, due to the lack of single-engine complex airplanes, the FAA has removed the 'complex' airplane requirement. Small single-engine complex planes never gained much popularity. They are more expensive to purchase and maintain, and the benefits they provide in terms of speed and fuel savings were just not attractive enough for private owners. Single-engine complex airplanes such as Cessna 172RG and Piper Arrow are still used in some flight schools, but currently only the Piper Arrow is still in production.

Most new single-engine trainers are not complex, but they are more technically advanced than older planes with analog instruments. Instead of using a complex plane in your training, you can substitute the ten-hour requirement to a 'technically advanced aircraft.'

FAA defines a technically advanced aircraft for commercial training purposes as an aircraft that has an electronic primary flight display, an electronic multi-function display, and a two-axis autopilot. These types of single-engine trainers are becoming more common in flight schools than single-engine complex planes. These types of advanced avionics can be installed in most new single-engine planes (such as Cessna 172s or Diamond DA40s) that are currently manufactured.

Complex Training

I did my initial complex training and my commercial checkride in a single-engine Cessna 172RG, which is a complex version of a Cessna 172 aircraft. Cessna hasn't produced the 172RGs since 1985, and the only single-engine complex training aircraft currently manufactured is the Piper Arrow. I never flew a Cessna 172RG after my commercial training, but I did instruct in Piper Arrows as a flight instructor.

Because of the recent rule change, you may never have a chance to fly a single-engine complex plane. You may, however, do most of your instrument and commercial training in one of those technically advanced airplanes. In this case, the last stage of your commercial training is likely to be just a review of everything you have already learned.

But if you do get to fly a complex plane, then you will get some fun experience. Flying a single-engine complex plane will also help your transition to a multi-engine aircraft that will be a complex plane for sure.

In a complex plane, you may have an additional control lever in the cockpit that you use to control the propeller blade angle. There are also additional engine instruments associated with the propeller speed. In some planes, the propeller angle may be controlled automatically, though. Another additional lever you will have to get used to is the landing gear lever that is accompanied with gear indicator lights.

The constant-speed or a variable pitch propeller of a complex plane is more efficient in producing thrust than a fixed pitch propeller. Also, the retractable landing gear reduces drag caused by the airframe and allows the airplane to fly faster and perform better. It will still be just a small, four-seat airplane, but it will feel more powerful.

A single-engine complex plane will handle just like any other single-engine plane in the air. But you will get to the training areas and back to the airport faster than before. You will also climb to altitudes faster, and you will notice significant altitude gains during maneuvers such as chandelles.

The biggest challenge in complex training at this point will be remembering different power settings and propeller settings as well as retracting and extending the landing gear at appropriate times. One of the most embarrassing (not to mention dangerous) things that can happen to a pilot is forgetting to lower the landing gear before landing!

In this stage, you will also learn how to act in case of malfunctions or emergencies relating to the new aircraft systems.

Technically Advanced Aircraft Training

If you train in a technically advanced aircraft (TAA) instead of a complex plane, then your training will be quite different. If you already did part of your training in an aircraft equipped with a Garmin G1000 or similar avionics package, then this will be easy training.

But if this is the first time you have electronic displays (also known as a glass cockpit), then the training is slightly more complicated. It takes some time to get used to flying with electronic instruments since they provide much more information than older analog instruments.

Having electronic flight displays and instruments in training planes is becoming more and more common. Training with these advanced avionics will help you with the transition to bigger planes that have modern instruments. But I would recommend you also learn to fly with older analog instruments as there are still many planes around that rely on those instruments. Moreover, you won't know for sure where your flight career takes you.

Having an autopilot in training airplanes is less common since you are supposed to learn to fly manually. But you will need to have an autopilot in addition to the electronic flight displays unless you have a complex plane available. It's certainly nice to have an autopilot available, especially when you do cross country flights, but during training, you are probably not going to use it that much. You will learn the different autopilot modes and the basic functions on how to use it during different phases of flights. Although, most of your flying will still be hand flying.

Multi-Engine Complex Training

You have another option to get the complex hours. It's possible to go straight into flying a multi-engine aircraft at this point. This is how we trained our commercial students in China because we didn't have single-engine complex planes available. The students did all their complex training and checkride in a twin-engine Diamond DA42 airplanes. Their training was paid by different airlines. And after graduation they had guaranteed airline jobs waiting for them, so in their case, there was no need for a single-engine commercial license.

If you do your complex training in a multi-engine

aircraft, you can also use the plane for your commercial checkride. Unfortunately, you would still have to do a single-engine checkride to be able to fly single-engine planes as a commercial pilot. Although, most airline jobs only fly multi-engine aircraft, it's still good to have a single-engine commercial license as well. You will need it to work as a flight instructor, fly sightseeing planes, fly passengers or cargo with single-engine planes such as Cessna Caravans. Moreover, you'll need it for many other general aviation jobs as well.

Doing all your complex training in a multi-engine aircraft might be more expensive than doing an add-on multi-engine rating later. But this is something you should discuss with your flight school. In the end, it doesn't matter which way you get your hours or what type of aircraft you use, just as long as you get quality training.

Final Stage Check and Commercial Pilot Practical Exam

Regardless of how you complete all your required training, there is usually a final stage check at the end of your training. Although, in Part 61 schools, you might simply proceed to the practical examination once your instructor determines you're ready for it.

Just like any final stage check, now it's your time to shine. It will be like a simulated checkride, so make sure you prepare for it properly. While this is a very important stage check, it may be easier than some of the other checks you have done so far.

By this time, you probably have an instrument rating added to your PPL certificate. And so, you are already skillful at handling the aircraft. This final stage check will be a VFR flight, so you will review everything you learned during your commercial flight training. The tough part is usually the oral exam, but it's easy to prepare for by using the CPL ACS as a checklist for preparation.

Once you pass the final stage check, it's time to take the commercial pilot practical examination as soon as possible, while everything is still fresh in your mind. You just need to double-check all your flight hours before scheduling the check. This ensures you meet all the requirements.

Because of the recent changes in the complex airplane requirements, it's better to check with your flight school or examiner that the airplane you are planning to use in the checkride is acceptable.

There seems to be a lot of confusion about this online. Based on the ACS, a complex plane is required for a multi-engine checkride, but not for a single-engine.

The aircraft needs to meet all the requirements by FAR 61.45.[6] If you train at a reputable 141 school, then you shouldn't have any worries. They will make sure you are trained in an aircraft that can be used in the checkride.

The practical exam will start with an oral exam, followed by the flight exam. Prepare for the oral exam just as you prepared for the final stage check. Make sure you review all the weak areas that you might have noticed during the final check.

You are now expected to explain things more in-depth than in your private pilot oral exam. You might have to explain more about aircraft systems and aerodynamics this time around. But more than likely, you will just spend more time explaining different regulations applying to commercial pilots. Don't worry too much about remembering every detail about everything you have learned. But make sure you know where to find the information if you forget something.

The flight part of the practical examination will be the easy part for most pilots. Just fly out there and do what you have been doing in the last several months! You'll be doing some VFR maneuvers, navigation, take-offs, landings, etc. All the maneuvers have to be done to commercial standards, which are stricter than private pilot standards. But this shouldn't be a problem at this stage. There shouldn't be any surprises as long as you received quality training.

If everything with the practical examination goes well, your examiner will sign you a temporary commercial pilot certificate on the spot. Congratulations! You can now work as a professional pilot! If you have a pilot job already lined up, you could start immediately. You could start flying small planes for sightseeing, cargo, aerial-photography, banner towing, etc.

Most jobs require more flight experience than just having a commercial pilot license, but you can still research and apply to whatever jobs are available. Maybe you'll get lucky.

But if you are like most pilots, you will continue your training the next day or the day after. Your initial commercial license only has a single-engine or multi-engine class rating in it. Next, you should add the missing rating for it, and it requires another checkride.

6

MULTI-ENGINE RATING

If you used a multi-engine aircraft for your complex training earlier, then it should be easy to add a multi-engine rating to your existing commercial pilot certificate. There is no need for an additional knowledge exam. You only need a practical examination for an additional aircraft class rating. So, if you are already proficient in multi-engine operations, then all you need is a multi-engine checkride right after you have received your single-engine commercial pilot certificate.

The more traditional route, however, is to do all commercial training in single-engine airplanes. Then, do separate multi-engine training. That's how I got my licenses. I finished my single-engine commercial checkride in a Cessna 172RG on November 11, 2000. I started my multi-engine training two days later.

I did my multi-engine training in a Piper Seminole PA-44. I only received 10.6 hours (ten hours and thirty-six minutes) of instruction, followed by a checkride on November 30. I could have done the whole rating in a week or so, but my instructor was busy with other students. I didn't get to fly every day, which is why it took me nearly three weeks.

The regulatory requirements for adding an aircraft class rating to your existing pilot license are described in FAR 61.63c.[1] As I already mentioned, there is no need for an additional knowledge test. Likewise, there is also no need to log specific amount of flight hours. Usually, ten to fifteen hours of training is enough.

You don't need as much training if you already have some complex plane experience. Some flight schools offer multi-engine add-on ratings to be done in only five days, but that may be rushing it. You will still need an instructor's endorsement before you can take the check-ride. To get that endorsement, you need to convince your instructor that you can safely operate the aircraft and meet all the requirements to pass the checkride. No instructor will sign you off if there is any doubt. After all, the instructor has to put his or her reputation and license on the line.

The training itself will focus on multi-engine operations described in the CPL ACS pages 57 - 60. You will
need to have a good understanding of all the knowledge
areas of multi-engine flying. The flight training will be
over fast, so make sure you study the knowledge areas.
Go through them with your instructor before you even
start flying.

Flying a multi-engine aircraft with all engines operating is as easy as single-engine flying. But things get
difficult if one engine of a twin-engine plane fails. As the
engines of most small twin-engine planes are mounted
on the wings, the airplane will immediately turn towards
the failed engine if you lose one. This requires imme-
diate and precise actions of the pilot.

In general, multi-engine airplanes are considered
safer than single-engine planes because they can still fly
if one engine fails. But without proper training and
understanding of multi-engine aerodynamics, it can be
easy for the pilot to lose control of the plane when an
engine fails. If you lose control of the aircraft even for a
second, things can get dangerous. That's why most of
your training will focus on single-engine operations
while flying a multi-engine airplane.

You will probably only fly about ten hours during
your training. But those will be very intense ten hours.
Your instructor will simulate engine failures in different

phases of flight, and you will be forced to properly secure failed the engine and fly the aircraft coordinated with only one engine operating.

Lots of rudder control will be required to fly the airplane with only one engine operating. You are going to learn to use rudders more than you ever did before. And your legs will be tired after every flight! Everything will, of course, be done in a controlled fashion; and, your instructor will be ready to help you at all times if necessary.

In your checkride, you won't be tested on the commercial maneuvers you already did in a single-engine aircraft. You will, however, be tested on one multi-engine specific demonstration: the Vmc Demonstration. Vmc stands for the minimum control speed with one engine inoperative. In aviation, "V" stands for speeds or velocities. Most common V-speeds such as Vy (best rate of climb), Vx (best angle of climb), Vs (stall speed), etc. you will actually learn already before your first flight lesson in your private pilot training. But you will get familiar with Vmc only during your multi-engine training.

There are several factors affecting the Vmc. For example, the position of flaps, landing gear, power lever, etc. affect the speed. If you slow the airplane down below this speed, you won't be able to maintain directional control anymore. As a result, the aircraft may spin and dive down from the sky.

It can be a very dangerous situation, which is why you will have to understand and be able to explain all the factors that affect this speed. You will also practice entering and recovering this situation during your training, and you will have to demonstrate it during your practical exam.

In addition to the Vmc demonstration and basic maneuvering with only one engine operating, you will have to do single-engine instrument approaches. This is when you really get to prove you can fly the plane coordinated!

The practical exam for an additional aircraft class rating is usually easier than the initial commercial examination. In the oral exam, you will just talk about aircraft specific things and multi-engine aerodynamics. During the exam's flight portion, you will normally just have to demonstrate the above-mentioned skills that you spend several hours practicing.

After you pass the checkride, you could relax a bit! Now you are a commercial pilot who can fly single- and multi-engine aircraft in instrument conditions! Feel free to apply for any pilot jobs available!

It is not unheard of for airlines to hire low-time first officers who then get more training in a simulator and on the job. If you do get a job as a low-time pilot, please be careful. Follow the rules because they are there for safety reasons. Keep educating yourself. Constantly learning about aviation helps, but won't replace actual flight experience. Be responsible, and know your limitations. And again, I would recommend you to stay in (flight) school a bit longer and get your flight instructor certificate next.

7

FLIGHT INSTRUCTOR CERTIFICATE FAR 61 SUBPART H AND FAR 141 APPENDIX F

A flight instructor certificate is technically not a pilot certificate. It's a completely separate FAA certificate, but you need to be a commercial pilot in order to become a Certified Flight Instructor (CFI).

Being a flight instructor is rarely a goal of anyone dreaming of becoming a pilot. But in many cases, it's the best option to gain flight experience early in pilot career. Instructing wasn't something I was looking forward to doing, but I'm glad I decided to do it.

I would never have guessed it, but I actually ended up enjoying teaching students to fly. Working as a flight instructor is still the most rewarding job I have ever had, not in terms of money and benefits, but in terms of satisfaction of job well done.

In my current job as a corporate pilot, my job is only to transport people from one place to another. It is not very life-changing to anyone. As a flight instructor though, you are changing the lives of the students you are teaching.

Once you have your commercial pilot certificate, it is in your best interest to spend a couple of more months (or less) on becoming a flight instructor. For the initial flight instructor certificate, you will need to receive forty hours of ground instruction and twenty-five hours of flight instruction if you train in a 141 school. The requirements will be less for additional instructor ratings. In 61 schools there are no specific flight hour or ground instruction hour requirements.

Certified Flight Instructor Ground School

The focus of the ground school will be on the fundamentals of instructing and the learning process. Essentially you will learn how to act as a teacher while learning to understand the best methods for teaching students.

It's great knowledge to have and will benefit you in your other studies as well. You could even use the knowledge and skills to help your children in their studies one day. In the ground school, you will cover everything from the FAA's Aviation Instructor Handbook.[1] You can download this for free anytime you want. It's an interesting read about human psychology, even if you are not planning to work as an instructor.

As a flight instructor, you will need to be knowledgeable about everything you learned during your private and commercial training. Now you will be expected to teach all that stuff. Not only you need to know how all the maneuvers are performed, but you will also need to have a clear understanding about *why* different maneuvers are practiced. And you need to be able to recognize common errors the students are likely to make while practicing each maneuver. When you understand the most common errors for each maneuver or situation, you can easily spot them and correct your students.

Certified Flight Instructor Knowledge Exams

You will have to take two knowledge exams to become a flight instructor – a fifty-question Fundamentals of Instructing Knowledge Exam and a hundred-question Flight Instructor Airplane Knowledge Exam. If you already hold a current teacher's certificate at a high school or higher level, you can receive credit towards the Fundamentals of Instructing Exam – skipping it altogether. You can learn more about the knowledge exams from the Flight and Ground Instructor Knowledge Test Guide.[2]

To prepare for the knowledge exams, I would recommend you use whatever study methods or online learning software you used until now.

Certified Flight Instructor Flight Training

Until this point, all your previous flight training should have been flying from the left seat while your instructor was sitting in the right seat. During instructor training, the roles are reversed.

Now you have to learn to fly from the right seat. It feels different at first, because now you will have to use a different hand for the flight controls, throttle, and everything else. Your viewing angle through the window will also be different. Flying visually with the reference to the horizon or landing on the centerline of the runway takes some adjusting. But it normally takes only a couple of flights to get the idea. Looking at the flight instruments will be different because they won't be in front of you anymore. Instead, you need to constantly look to the left when you fly by the instruments. You will practice all the PPL and CPL maneuvers up to commercial standards while flying from the right seat. The required twenty-five flight hours are usually more than enough to get used to the right seat flying.

Learning to fly from the right seat is, of course, not all you have to do. The flight training to become a flight instructor is like role-playing. You will pretend to be the instructor during the flights, and your instructor will pretend to be a student with no flight experience. You will teach your instructor by explaining how everything is done. When you practice different maneuvers, you will constantly have to explain what you are doing. Point out everything you are looking at during each maneuver or during each phase of flight. After you demonstrate each maneuver, you will ask your 'student' to do them. Your instructor, who is acting as a student, is likely to do some mistakes or common errors on purpose that you should recognize and point out.

It may feel weird at first to be teaching someone who already knows how to fly, but you just have to play the game and pretend that you are the instructor. Even though your instructing may feel forced, you need to keep in mind that it's necessary and useful training for your benefit. Later on, working as a flight instructor and giving instruction is actually easier when you know you have the actual authority to give instruction and knowledge to share with your students.

Certified Flight Instructor Practical Examination

The initial CFI practical exam can be easy or difficult, depending on your examiner. You are expected to know a lot more things than a private or a commercial pilot — and you are expected to know how to teach that knowledge.

But with proper preparation, you shouldn't have much to worry about. The best way to prepare is by using the Flight Instructor Practical Test Standards (CFI PTS) booklet as a study checklist.[3]

Once you pass the initial CFI checkride, you can legally instruct private and commercial pilot students. You are limited to VFR training only while flying with commercial students. In order to teach instrument and multi-engine students, you would need to add additional ratings to your CFI license. Normally the next step for new flight instructors is getting an instrument rating added to their flight instructor certificate.

Certified Flight Instructor Instrument Rating

You need to prove yourself to an FAA examiner again if you want to teach students for their instrument rating or do instrument training for commercial students. There are separate Practical Test Standards published for Certified Flight Instructor Instrument (CFII PTS).[4]

As a new flight instructor, you probably start initially teaching private pilot students. In this case, you might feel as if you don't need the CFII certificate. However, I recommend that you get the CFII rating added as soon as possible after getting your initial CFI checkride done.

Without the instrument rating, you may miss out on some instrument and commercial students who might otherwise be assigned to you as you work as a flight instructor. Also, if you decide not to get it initially, but need the rating later, it will be very frustrating to become a student again when you should be the one instructing. It's better get all your certificates and ratings done before you get busy working as a flight instructor.

FAR Part 141 training programs require fifteen hours of ground training and fifteen hours flight training from CFII applicants. I think that is quite a lot, especially if you get the rating immediately after you are done with your initial CFI training. Some of the training can be done in flight training devices or full flight simulators, though, which can reduce the cost of the rating.

If you train under 61 rules, there are no specific time requirements. I started my CFII training a couple of days after I passed my initial flight instructor checkride. Although I did all my training in a 141 school, the CFII training was done under FAR Part 61 rules. I was still in the same 141 school and using the same airplanes. I just didn't follow a 141 curriculum. I only did five flights, totaling 5.3 hours (five hours and eighteen minutes) of flight time until I was ready for the checkride. It was much cheaper than paying for fifteen hours of flight training and fifteen hours of ground training!

Once again, you will have to do a computerized knowledge exam before you can do the practical exam. The knowledge exam for Instrument Instructor Rating[5] has fifty questions, and you have two and a half hours to complete it. It's good to get this exam completed way in advance. I would get it done before you even start your instrument instructor training.

Of course, if you follow a 141 curriculum with fifteen hours of ground training, then you should do the written exam at the end of the course with an endorsement from your ground instructor. If you do the training under 61 rules, then you'll need an endorsement from your instructor or proof that you have completed one of the online study courses I mentioned earlier in this book.

The CFII flight training is similar to what you had to do during your initial CFI training. You will be flying from the right seat while explaining everything you do to your instructor, who is pretending to be a student on the left seat. Instead of doing VFR maneuvers, you will be doing basic attitude instrument flying, instrument approaches, holding procedures, and other instrument procedures.

CFII checkride is usually easier than the initial CFI checkride. It's especially easy if you do it with the same FAA examiner soon after you complete the initial check. This way, it's unlikely that the examiner will grill you with the same questions about fundamentals of instructing and such. You will just focus on explaining different instrument procedures in the oral exam, and if your previous oral exam went well, then this time around should be quick.

During the flight part of the exam, you will have to 'teach' the examiner some basic instrument flying, holding procedures, instrument approaches, etc. Basically you do the same procedures that you did in your instrument checkride. Except this time, you will fly from the right seat.

The CFII checkride was my last flight in the South Carolina training school. My next flight was an instructor checkout flight in a Florida flight school, where I started my first job as a flight instructor. I got the job only about two weeks after my graduation from the professional pilot training program in South Carolina. At the time, I was eager to change the scenery and start working as a flight instructor. Later, I regretted that I didn't spend an extra week or two in South Carolina and get my Multi-Engine Instructor (MEI) rating while I was still there.

Getting the MEI is the next step if you plan to work as a flight instructor for a while, and want to accumulate some valuable multi-engine experience at the same time.

Multi-Engine Instructor

MEI training is usually not included in the up-front costs of any professional pilot training programs. So if you want the rating, you will most likely have to pay for it separately. In my experience, most pilots only plan to work as flight instructors for a short time and never bother getting the MEI.

Many small flight schools don't even have multi-engine airplanes. So, if you plan to work for such flight school, your MEI rating may go to waste. Also, the multi-engine training is usually such a small part of students' training that many instructors may feel they won't get to do much multi-engine instructing anyway.

The flight school where I ended up working as a new flight instructor didn't do much multi-engine training. So, I don't think I missed many multi-engine flight opportunities without the MEI. Although, I believe having it would have made my life easier later.

I decided to get the MEI a couple of years after getting my initial CFI license. It wasn't easy because I had only done a couple of multi-engine flights since getting my initial multi-engine rating.

Also, I ended up doing the MEI in a different type of airplane — one of which I had never flown before. It would have been much easier and cheaper to get it done soon after I got my initial CFI and CFII licenses because I could have done it in a familiar airplane in familiar environment.

I got the MEI at the time basically just to stay current with my flight skills, and in case I needed it in the future. I didn't get it because I needed it for a job at the time. Although, it turns out that it came in handy when I moved to China. Thanks to the license, I was able to work as a multi-engine instructor and a chief flight instructor gaining valuable flight experience. I got to fly brand new Diamond DA42 Twin Stars for over 400 hours in China, which in turn, helped me get a job in corporate aviation.

Of course, many flight instructors have proceeded with their careers to bigger planes without ever getting the MEI. But it can help you get some multi-engine time early in your career if you end up working in a flight school that has a fleet of multi-engine airplanes.

It's definitely a rating you should consider getting

early on and treat it as an investment to advance your career faster. Plus, getting to fly more different types of airplanes makes your career as a pilot much more fun!

Multi-Engine Instructor Flight Training

There are no flight hour requirements for MEI training set forth by the FAA. Except, different flight schools may dictate specific hour requirements in their training programs. Usually, ten to fifteen hours of flight training should be enough.

It's merely an add-on rating to your CFI license, so you won't have to complete all the tasks in the different areas of operations described in the CFI PTS. You will mostly just practice and be tested on all the multi-engine operations. Page ninety-seven of the CFI PTS has a table that shows the areas of operations required for adding a multi-engine rating to a flight instructor certificate.

As a multi-engine instructor, you will have to do everything you did for your multi-commercial rating from the right seat. There is only one additional task that you need to learn — the drag demonstration.

"Demonstrating the Effects of Various Airspeeds and Configurations During Engine Inoperative Performance" is required by the PTS, more commonly known as the drag demonstration. As the name implies, you will have to demonstrate how different configurations and airspeeds affect the airplane's single-engine flight characteristics. Basically, the demonstration is done by reducing one engine power to idle. Then, lowering the flaps and landing gear down one-by-one while observing and pointing out the effects to the airspeed.

Once you get this rating, you are all good to go for a profitable career as a flight instructor! Okay, maybe not that profitable, but it will be a fun and exciting job for sure!

8

GROUND INSTRUCTOR CERTIFICATE — FAR 61 SUBPART I AND FAR 141 APPENDIX H

Obviously, your goal is to work as a pilot flying airplanes instead of working in an office or teaching in front of a classroom. But if you decided to get a flight instructor certificate, you can very easily get a ground instructor certificate as well.

All you need to do is complete a computer-based knowledge exam. This will provide you with a ground instructor certificate. You can use it to make a living in case you lose your pilot license or medical certificate for any reason. Think of it as a cheap and easy loss-of-license insurance policy.

There are three different levels of ground instructor certificates:

- **Basic Ground Instructor (BGI)**
  Required to provide ground instruction for sport, recreational, and private pilot students.
- **Advanced Ground Instructor (AGI)**
  Required for providing ground training towards all other pilot certificates except the instrument rating.
- **Instrument Ground Instructor (IGI)**
  Required to provide ground training towards the instrument rating.

As a BGI, you can only provide very basic training up to a private pilot level. If you take the AGI exam, you won't need to do the BGI exam. As an advanced ground instructor, you can teach PPL students as well.

Becoming a BGI is not a pre-requisite for becoming an advanced ground instructor. So, there is really no point for anyone to take the BGI exam. It's so limiting, so it's better just go for the advanced ground instructor certificate immediately.

I took the AGI and IGI knowledge exams when I was doing my flight instructor training. With the ground instructor certificates, I can provide classroom instruction to pilot students and endorse them for their written exams.

You don't even have to be a pilot to become a ground instructor. If you are passionate about aviation (but for some reason can't become a pilot), you can still get a ground instructor certificate and teach the theory of aviation to pilot students. If you are motivated enough and given an opportunity, you could even work as a ground instructor while you are taking flight lessons.

To become a ground instructor in a 141 school, you will need twenty hours ground instruction toward the initial certificate and ten hours for additional ratings. Under 61 rules, there won't be any hour requirements. A 61 school is the way to go, especially if you are not immediately planning on working as a ground instructor. No point in paying for all those ground school hours if you are not even planning to use the certificates until you retire from flying!

You will need to take separate knowledge exams for each of the ground instructor certificate levels. For basic instructor, the exam has eighty questions, while an advanced instructor exam has a hundred questions. The instrument instructor exam has fifty questions. But like I said, there is no need to take the basic ground instructor exam. Just do the advanced and instrument instructor exams, and you can teach students for all licenses. No practical or oral exam is required for a ground instructor certificate.

To study for the exams, I recommend you use the same study methods or study guides you used for all the other certificates. If you haven't researched different online courses yet, a good one to check out is the Gleim aviation online ground school. [1]

It's good to have a ground instructor certificate, because you never know when you might need it. There is no expiration date on the certificate, although there are some requirements to stay current with your knowledge in order to exercise your ground instructor privileges. In any case, if you are planning to work as a flight instructor, you might as well get the ground instructor certificate to make yourself more marketable!

Ready to Be a Flight / Ground Instructor?

With all the flight and ground instructor certificates under your belt, you are ready to face the challenges of teaching brand new pilot students. I worked as a flight instructor on and off for several years in the United States. Likewise, I worked for five years as a full-time flight instructor in China. Three of those years I was the chief flight instructor of a major flight school in China. I have worked in four different flight schools and trained hundreds of students at all levels of training — from private pilots to flight instructors with multi-engine and instrument ratings.

I worked as a regular flight instructor, check instructor, assistant chief flight instructor, and as the chief flight instructor. Needless to say, I have many exciting stories to share from my instructor career. It is not in the scope of this book to talk about those experiences, but my next book will talk about working as a flight instructor. For updates about the Pilot Career Series Book 3 please, please **sign up for my email list**.

Next Steps

Of all the certificates and ratings I have described so far, you should get each of them one after the other. In most cases, it would be in your best interest to stay in one training school until you get all of them. That's especially true if you are planning to work as a flight instructor as your first pilot job. However, if you have an entry-level pilot job lined up, doing something else other than flight instructing, might make you want to skip all the flight and ground instructor certificates.

A commercial pilot license can get you far with your flight career, but there will come a time when you need to do more training. As a commercial pilot, you can work as a pilot in command for commuter or non-scheduled (charter) airlines. But if you want to work as a captain for any major airlines operating under FAR 121 rules (rules that major airlines have to follow), you will need to obtain an Airline Transport Pilot (ATP) certificate.

Although not regulatory, most companies operating turbojet airplanes require an airline pilot license from their captains, which is the reason I had to get my ATP. Even though I work in corporate aviation instead of passenger airlines.

You won't need the ATP anytime soon after you get your commercial license initially. In fact, you will need to log at least 1500 hours of total flight time before you can even apply for it — and there are other requirements. Of course, it is good to get it done as soon as you meet the requirements. And so, I will briefly talk about the ATP requirements next.

9

AIRLINE TRANSPORT PILOT CERTIFICATE — FAR 61 SUBPART G AND FAR 141 APPENDIX E

I got my airline transport pilot license (ATPL) nearly seventeen years after I got my commercial pilot license. I had no use for it earlier because I didn't follow the airline career route. Instead, I stayed in general and corporate aviation. I'm glad I got it eventually, because it provides me with many more job opportunities – should I ever want to find a new job.

You certainly shouldn't wait seventeen years to get your ATPL. It's better to get it as soon as you meet the flight experience requirements and when it is practicable for you. But until you meet the requirements, you shouldn't worry about it.

The aeronautical experience hour requirements for ATPL are as follows:

- Total of 1500 flight hours including:
- 500 of cross-country flight time.
- One hundred hours of night flight time.
- Fifty hours in the class of airplane for the rating sought.
- Seventy-five hours of actual or simulated instrument flight time.
- 250 hours as pilot in command (PIC) or as a second in command (SIC) under the supervision of the PIC. These 250 hours should further include at least: One hundred hours of cross-country flight time and twenty-five hours night flight time.

The detailed aeronautical experience requirements can be found from FAR 61.159.[1] For me, and for many other flight instructors, the most difficult requirement was to get the 500 hours of cross-country flight time.

As a flight instructor, you don't get to do many cross-country flights because most of the training is done near your base airport. The cross-country requirement is not difficult to meet if you get to work in any cargo or passenger transport job. Typically, all those flights are cross-country flights.

All the other flight time requirements are normally easy to obtain within the 1500 hours of total flight time.

The Airline Transport Pilot Certification Training Program

There is some ground training and a knowledge a exam involved in getting the ATPL. Before you can take the knowledge exam, you need to complete a seven-day Airline Transport Pilot Certification Training Program (ATP-CTP) course which is required by the FAA.

The course itself is very easy because there is no practical examination or knowledge examination involved. Well, there is a short multiple-choice exam that you have to take, just so there will be a record showing you have completed the course — but the course cannot be failed.

The purpose of the course is to prepare you to transition from piston planes to jet aircraft. However, you will still have to do it, even if you have been flying jet aircraft for years. I took the course after flying nearly six years in a Challenger jet.

There are only a few locations[2] in the United States where you can take the course. The course costs about $5000, and it includes some training in a full-motion jet aircraft simulator.

Because of the time, cost, and locations of the training centers, it's usually not very convenient for many pilots to take the course. In many cases, it might be better to wait for your company to pay for it and let them arrange the training for you. My company arranged the training for me so that I could fly a US registered aircraft in China as the pilot in command. Everyone except one of the six students in my ATP-CTP class was there on their company dime as well.

Airline Transport Pilot Knowledge Exam

Once you complete the course, you can schedule the ATP knowledge exam. Only one written exam is required by the FAA, while in Europe you would have to take fourteen separate exams. There are 125 questions in the computerized FAA ATP exam. It is very easy if you use one of the online training courses, such as the one provided by Sheppard Air. I got ninety-nine percent correct in my exam by following their study method. You still have to put some effort into studying for it, but it's nothing to stress about.

Airline Transport Pilot Practical Examination

You can then take the practical exam once you have taken the ATP knowledge exam. I did my ATP practical examination at the end of my regular re-current training for the Challenger 605. The checkride will cover all the requirements described in the Airline Transport Pilot and Type Rating for Airplane — Airman Certification Standards (ATP ACS).[3]

The practical exam will again have an oral exam and a flight exam. In the oral exam, you will mostly have to answer questions about the system's specific to the aircraft in which you are flying. That is especially true if you do the practical exam at the end of recurrent training. If you don't have any multi-crew experience at this time, then you will probably discuss many aspects of crew resource management and airline pilot regulations with the examiner.

Most airline transport pilots that I have met have done the ATP checkride in a full-motion flight simulator representing the aircraft have already been flying for years. It's usually the easiest way to do it. If you have more than one type of rating in your commercial pilot license at the time, all of them will be transferred to your new ATP license upon passing the checkride.

You can, of course, do the flight part in any aircraft that satisfies the ACS's requirements. I know pilots who have done the ATP checkride in small twin planes like the Piper Seminole or Seneca. If you build your flight hours as a flight instructor, for example, getting the ATP done (even in a small aircraft you are used to flying) would be a good way to go. It would help your chances of getting an airline or corporate pilot job later on.

The airline transport pilot certificate is technically the last pilot certificate you need to get in order for a life-long pilot career. But your studies won't end there, and the ATP checkride won't be your last checkride.

Aircraft Type Ratings

Most large aircraft and turbojet-powered aircraft require a separate type rating. Aircraft type ratings can be added to your ATP or CPL license, as they define what types of aircraft you are allowed to fly as a pilot in command. Training for a type rating takes typically about a month of full-time training.

You may end up flying one type of aircraft for many years, but depending on your specific circumstances, you may get to do several type ratings during your career. Most airline pilots start their careers with smaller passenger transportation turboprops or jets, later advancing into bigger jets. There is a practical examination, and usually, a written examination, involved with each type rating. It's very similar to what was involved in getting each certificate so far.

Re-current Training

You will further have to do regular re-current training for all the type ratings you want to maintain up-to-date. Re-current training is usually done once or twice a year, depending on the company for which you work. The purpose of the training is to practice emergency and abnormal procedures that you don't normally do during daily flights. Re-current training ensures that pilots are prepared to face the challenges of unexpected emergencies such as engine failures, fires, sudden depressurization, or pilot incapacitations. The training usually takes five to seven days. It involves ground school, simulator training, written examination, oral exam and a flight exam – all the fun stuff again and again! That's a pilot career for you!

It may sound intimidating to do so frequent training and testing, but it gets easier with experience. And, it's important training to keep us all safe in the skies. Thanks to all the training we do, airline accidents are very infrequent these days. Flying is still the safest method of transportation there is!

I kept this Airline Transport Pilot section relatively short on purpose. At the beginning of your flight career, it's good for you to know what kind of training and certificates you will need to obtain in the future. But at this point, a detailed description of the training and requirements won't make any difference.

I will discuss more of how I got my ATP certificates (one from China, one from the United States, and hopefully one from Europe soon) and my jet aircraft type ratings in the Pilot Career Series Book 4. In that book, I will talk about my experiences as a corporate jet pilot and working in a multi-crew environment. For updates about my upcoming books please, please sign up via the link at the end of the book.

10

OTHER RATINGS

What I have described so far in this book is everything that you will ever need for an awesome career as a professional pilot.

Now, if you are interested in expanding your horizons a bit, there are countless aircraft categories and ratings that you might want to pursue depending on the opportunities available to you.

Two additional ratings available to your airplane license are singe- and multi-engine seaplane ratings. I got my single-engine seaplane rating back in 2007. It was the most fun flying I have ever done, but unfortunately, I have never had the opportunity to fly seaplanes ever since. There are not that many seaplane jobs available, but if you live near a seaplane base, by all means, try to get that rating!

Other aircraft categories include things like gliders, balloons, helicopters, etc. There are lots of opportunities in aviation. Although, airplane pilots usually have the best career advancement opportunities.

I'm not going into the details of all the other certificates and ratings since most pilots don't ever need them. I just wanted to mention them, so you know what's out there.

If you get your multi-engine commercial pilot license with an instrument rating, you are in an excellent position for a life-long pilot career! Just remember there are many other pilot jobs and opportunities in case a typical fixed-wing airplane pilot career doesn't interest you.

FINAL WORDS

Did you enjoy this book?

If this book somehow inspired you to pursue a pilot career or if you otherwise enjoyed reading it, I would like to ask you a small favor. I would appreciate it very much if you could leave me a review on Amazon, Goodreads, or any other book review website that you prefer.

In Amazon or Goodreads, simply type in my name (Vesa Turpeinen), then choose this book to leave a review.

That would help other aspiring pilots or readers interested in the subject to find this book. Even a sentence or two would be very helpful!

Join my Facebook group!

Remember to also join me and other aspiring pilots at my Pilot Career Facebook Group (facebook.com/groups/pilotcareers/). There you can get more personalized advice based on your circumstances.

Do you have questions or comments?

If you have any further questions or comments about the topics covered in this book, you can send me an email at vesa.turpeinen@funkypilot.com.

I wish you the best of luck with your pilot career!

Happy Flying, Everyone!

...AND ONE MORE THING

The purpose of this book was to give you an idea of what to expect from your time as a pilot student. I highly recommend you get a flight instructor license to gain some initial flight experience. If you feel as if you don't know what flight instructing is all about, please stay tuned for my next book.

In my next book, *"**Pilot Career Book 3**,"* I will talk about my time as a flight instructor, working myself up to a chief flight instructor of a 141 school. I have many exciting stories from those times that I think you will find entertaining, inspirational, yet educational.

Sign up here: **funkypilot.com/bonus2** for updates

about my next books. Then you'll get notified when the books are available for pre-sale, so you can get them for the lowest price.

www.funkypilot.com

A SPECIAL FREE GIFT FOR YOU!

As a THANK YOU for purchasing my book, I would like to give you FREE instant access to some bonus materials. The bonus materials include the following:

- Phonetic Alphabet for Pilots — Cheatsheet.
- Decoding Guide for METAR and TAF Weather Reports

Get your bonus materials here:
www.funkypilot.com/bonus2

GLOSSARY

- AC — Advisory Circular
- ACS — Airman Certification Standards
- ADM — Aeronautical Decision Making
- AFM — Airplane (or Aircraft) Flight Manual
- AGI — Advanced Ground Instructor
- AIM — Aeronautical Information Manual
- AOPA — Aircraft Owners and Pilots Association
- ASA — Aviation Supplies and Academics
- ATC — Air Traffic Control
- ATP — Airline Transport Pilot

- ATP CTP — Airline Transport Pilot Certification Training Program
- ATPL — Airline Transport Pilot License
- BGI — Basic Ground Instructor
- CAAC — Civil Aviation Administration of China
- CFI — Certified Flight Instructor
- CFII — Certified Flight Instructor Instrument
- CFR — Code of Federal Regulations
- CPL — Commercial Pilot Licence
- CRM — Crew Resource Management
- DME — Distance Measuring Equipment
- eCFR — Electronic Code of Federal Regulations
- EASA — European Aviation Safety Agency
- ETA — Estimated Time of Arrival
- FAA — Federal Aviation Administration
- FAR — Federal Aviation Regulations
- FSDO — Flight Standards District Office
- GPS — Global Positioning System
- IACRA — Integrated Airman Certification and Rating Application
- IFR — Instrument Flight Rules
- IGI — Instrument Ground Instructor
- ILS — Instrument Landing System

- IMC — Instrument Meteorological Conditions
- IPC — Instrument Proficiency Check
- IR — Instrument Rating
- LDA — Localizer Type Directional Aid
- LOC — Localizer
- MDA — Minimum Descent Altitude
- MEI — Multi-Engine Instructor
- METAR — Meteorological Terminal Aviation Routine Weather Report
- NAS — National Airspace System
- NDB — Non-directional Radio Beacon
- NTSB — National Transportation Safety Board
- PAR — Precision Approach Radar
- PHAK — Pilot's Handbook of Aeronautical Knowledge
- PIC — Pilot in Command
- POH — Pilot Operating Handbook
- PPL — Private Pilot License
- PTS — Practical Test Standards
- RNAV — Area Navigations
- SIC — Second in Command
- SID — Standard Instrument Departure
- STAR — Standard Instrument Arrival Procedures

- TAA — Technically Advanced Aircraft
- TAF — Terminal Area Forecast
- VFR — Visual Flight Rules
- Vmc — Minimum Control Speed
- VMC — Visual Meteorological Conditions
- VOR — Very-High Frequency (VHF) Omni-Directional Range
- Vx — Best Angle of Climb
- Vy — Best Rate of Climb

NOTES

About This Book

1. Pilot Career Series Book 1: https://www.amazon.com/dp/B07QJBLCPG
2. Example Endnote
3. Pilot Career Resources: https://www.funkypilot.com/resources

2. Student Pilot Certificate - FAR 61 Subpart C

1. Information about FAA student pilot certificates: https://www.faa.gov/pilots/become/student_cert/
2. Integrated Airman Certification and Rating Application (IACRA): https://iacra.faa.gov/IACRA/Default.aspx

3. Private Pilot Certificate - FAR 61 Subpart E and FAR 141 Appendix B

1. Electronic Code of Federal Regulations (eCFR): https://www.ecfr.gov/cgi-bin/text-idx?SID=50b4b4e7015c3c1227f2acb707e792bb&mc=true&tpl=/ecfrbrowse/Title14/14tab_02.tpl
2. 14 CFR (FAR) Part 61: https://www.ecfr.gov/cgi-bin/text-idx?SID=50b4b4e7015c3c1227f2acb707e792bb&mc=true&node=pt14.2.61&rgn=div5
3. FAR Part 141: https://www.ecfr.gov/cgi-bin/text-idx?SID=

50b4b4e7015c3c1227f2acb707e792bb&mc=true&node=pt14.3.141&rgn=div5#sp14.3.141.b

4. FAR Part 91: https://www.ecfr.gov/cgi-bin/text-idx?SID=43229fd68eeab-b4d8f2d23b2de6f70f7&mc=true&node=pt14.2.91&rgn=div5

5. 49 CFR Part 830 (Accident and Incident Reporting to NTSB): https://www.ecfr.gov/cgi-bin/text-idx?SID=9966a067f99b1ae30beddfa717b7e055&mc=true&node=pt49.7.830&rgn=div5

6. Funkypilot Resources / FAA Manuals: https://funkypilot.com/resources/

7. AC 61.65H Certification: Pilots and Flight and Ground Instructors: https://www.faa.gov/documentLibrary/media/Advisory_Circular/AC_61-65H.pdf

8. FAA Advisory Circulars (AC): https://www.faa.gov/regulations_policies/advisory_circulars/

9. Sample Radio Calls from AOPA: https://www.aopa.org/-/media/files/aopa/home/pilot-resources/asi/sampleradiocalls.pdf

10. FunkyPilot Resources / Pilot's Handbook of Aeronautical Knowledge: https://funkypilot.com/resources/

11. PHAK Chapter 12: https://www.faa.gov/regulations_policies/handbooks_manuals/aviation/phak/media/14_phak_ch12.pdf

12. PHAK Chapter 13: https://www.faa.gov/regulations_policies/handbooks_manuals/aviation/phak/media/15_phak_ch13.pdf

13. Flight Computers: https://funkypilot.com/resources/

14. Weight and Balance Handbook: https://www.faa.gov/regulations_policies/handbooks_manuals/aviation/media/FAA-H-8083-1.pdf

    Or: https://funkypilot.com/resources/

15. Spin Training Video from China: https://funkypilot.com/2018/01/28/flight-experience-5-1-spinning-a-diamond-da20-in-china/

16. The Highest Duty: My Search for What Really Matters: https://funkypilot.com/book-recommendations/

17. Electronic Code of Federal Regulations: https://www.ecfr.gov

18. FAR/AIM by ASA: https://funkypilot.com/resources/

19. Private Pilot Airman Certification Standards (PPL ACS): https://www.faa.gov/training_testing/testing/acs/media/private_airplane_acs_change_1.pdf

20. Aircraft Owners and Pilots Association (AOPA): https://www.aopa.org

21. Gleim Aviation: https://www.gleimaviation.com

22. Sporty's Pilot Shop: https://www.sportys.com

23. FAA Testing Resources: https://www.faa.gov/training_testing/testing/

24. Locate a Testing Center: http://candidate.catstest.com/sitesearch.php

25. Private Pilot Knowledge Test Guide: https://www.faa.gov/training_testing/testing/test_guides/media/FAA-G-8082-17I.pdf

26. FAR Part 1 — Definitions and Abbreviations: https://www.ecfr.gov/cgi-bin/text-idx?SID=4201e5b0cd884525e76df29636c1b240&mc=true&node=se14.1.1_11&rgn=div8

27. Airplane Flying Handbook: https://www.faa.gov/regulations_policies/handbooks_manuals/aviation/airplane_handbook/media/airplane_flying_handbook.pdf

28. ASA Oral Exam Guides / FunkyPilot Flight Training: https://funkypilot.com/aviation/flight-training/

4. Instrument Rating - FAR 61.65 and FAR 141 Appendix C

1. FAR 61.65 Instrument Rating Requirements: https://www.ecfr.gov/cgi-bin/text-idx?SID=eaba499e6ced308adb88b36dae4e464f&mc=true&node=se14.2.61_165&rgn=div8

2. FAR 141 Appendix C — Instrument Rating Course: https://www.ecfr.gov/cgi-bin/text-idx?SID=eaba499e6ced308adb88b36dae4e464f&mc=true&node=pt14.

3.141&rgn=div5#ap14.3.141.0000_onbspnbspnbsp.c

3. FAR 91.167 - 91.193 Instrument Flight Rules: https://www.ecfr.gov/cgi-bin/text-idx?SID=eaba499e6ced308adb88b36dae4e464f&mc=true&node=pt14.3.141&rgn=div5#ap14.3.141.0000_onbspnbspnbsp.c

4. Aeronautical Information Manual (AIM): https://www.faa.gov/air_traffic/publications/media/aim_basic_chgs_1-3_2-28-19.pdf

5. Instrument Flying Handbook: https://www.faa.gov/regulations_policies/handbooks_manuals/aviation/media/FAA-H-8083-15B.pdf

6. Instrument Procedures Handbook: https://www.faa.gov/regulations_policies/handbooks_manuals/aviation/instrument_procedures_handbook/

7. Advanced Avionics Handbook: https://www.faa.gov/regulations_policies/handbooks_manuals/aviation/advanced_avionics_handbook/

8. Instrument Rating Airman Certification Standards: https://www.faa.gov/training_testing/testing/acs/media/instrument_rating_acs_change_1.pdf

9. Jeppesen Instrument / Commercial Handbook: https://funkypilot.com/aviation/flight-training/

10. Sheppard Air online courses: http://sheppardair.com

11. Instrument Rating Knowledge Test Guide: https://www.faa.gov/training_testing/testing/test_guides/media/FAA-G-8082-13I.pdf

12. View Limiting Devices for Instrument Training: https://funkypilot.com/aviation/flight-training/

13. Instrument Patterns: https://www.gleim.com/public/pdf/av_updates/ipfmadd2.pdf

14. Holding Pattern Entries: https://www.aopa.org/news-and-media/all-news/2019/june/flight-training-magazine/technique-instrument-holds

15. Oral Exam Guides: https://funkypilot.com/aviation/flight-training/

16. eCFR 61.57 - Recent Flight Experience: Pilot in Command:

https://www.ecfr.gov/cgi-bin/text-idx?SID=
f5b7d93289a704728b3417d211d70e85&mc=true&node=
pt14.2.61&rgn=div5#se14.2.61_157

5. Commercial Pilot Certificate - FAR 61 Subpart F and FAR 141 Appendix D

1. FAR Part 61, Subpart F — Commercial Pilots: https://www.ecfr.
   gov/cgi-bin/text-idx?SID=
   56b5d1e10240d524cadaa2526eda6351&mc=true&node=pt14.
   2.61&rgn=div5#sp14.2.61.f
2. Commercial Pilot Knowledge Test Guide: https://www.faa.gov/
   training_testing/testing/test_guides/media/FAA-G-8082-
   5H.pdf
3. Commercial Pilot Airman Certification Standards: https://www.
   faa.gov/training_testing/testing/acs/media/
   commercial_airplane_acs_change_1.pdf
4. FAR 61.129 — Commercial Pilots: https://www.ecfr.gov/cgi-
   bin/text-idx?SID=21646614b36555a853a70740060d1fac&
   mc=true&node=se14.2.61_1129&rgn=div8
5. FAR 141 Appendix D — Commercial Pilots: http://www.ecfr.
   gov/cgi-bin/text-idx?SID=
   21646614b36555a853a70740060d1fac&mc=true&node=pt14.
   3.141&rgn=div5#ap14.3.141.0000_onbspnbspnbsp.d
6. FAR 61.45 Practical Tests: Required Aircraft and Equipment:
   https://www.ecfr.gov/cgi-bin/text-idx?SID=
   c94e58030707e6a285535bed28d3ab5b&mc=true&node=se14.
   2.61_145&rgn=div8

6. Multi-Engine Rating

1. FAR 61.63c — Additional Ratings: https://www.ecfr.gov/cgi-bin/text-idx?SID=59bb4146f37ff560a154ff468c74c1e6&mc=true&node=se14.2.61_163&rgn=div8

7. Flight Instructor Certificate FAR 61
Subpart H and FAR 141 Appendix F

1. Aviation Instructor Handbook: https://www.faa.gov/regulations_policies/handbooks_manuals/aviation/aviation_instructors_handbook/media/FAA-H-8083-9A.pdf
2. Flight and Ground Instructor Knowledge Test Guide: https://www.faa.gov/training_testing/testing/test_guides/media/FAA-G-8082-7I.pdf
3. Flight Instructor Practical Test Standards: https://www.faa.gov/training_testing/testing/test_standards/media/FAA-S-8081-6D.pdf
4. Instrument Instructor Practical Test Standards: https://www.faa.gov/training_testing/testing/test_standards/media/FAA-S-8081-9D.pdf
5. Instrument Instructor Knowledge Test Guide: https://www.faa.gov/training_testing/testing/test_guides/media/FAA-G-8082-13I.pdf

8. Ground Instructor Certificate — FAR 61
Subpart I and FAR 141 Appendix H

1. Gleim Aviation online ground school: https://www.gleimaviation.com/flight-instructors/

9. Airline Transport Pilot Certificate — FAR 61 Subpart G and FAR 141 Appendix E

1. FAR 61.159 Aeronautical Experience requirements for airline pilots: https://www.ecfr.gov/cgi-bin/text-idx?SID= b9d7ebe61a7c7eco8b195e1991c96ced&mc=true&node=pt14. 2.61&rgn=div5#se14.2.61_1159

2. ATP CTP Course Locations: https://www.faa.gov/pilots/ training/atp/media/ATP_CTP_Providers.pdf

3. ATP ACS: https://www.faa.gov/training_testing/testing/acs/ media/atp_acs.pdf

ABOUT THE AUTHOR

Vesa Turpeinen is a longtime aviator, pilot, and flight instructor. He is the former Chief Flight Instructor of the Chaoyang Flight College of CAUC and MBA graduate from Embry-Riddle Aeronautical University. Vesa grew up in Helsinki, Finland, and currently resides in Hangzhou, China.

This is Vesa's second published book, and more of his aviation series will follow. Meanwhile, he welcomes everyone to read his stories in his aviation and travel blog: funkypilot.com.

Other books by Vesa Turpeinen:

THE PILOT CAREER SERIES - BOOK I

LEARN TO FLY AND
BECOME A PILOT !

The Ultimate Guide for Determining Your
Capabilities of Becoming a Professional Pilot
and Getting Started with Flight Training

VESA TURPEINEN

Made in the USA
Columbia, SC
06 October 2020